T0077890

Strivings

Life, Learning, and Purpose

STUART I. FORMAN

Archway Publishing books may be ordered through booksellers or by contacting:

Archway Publishing
1663 Liberty Drive
Bloomington, IN 47403
www.archwaypublishing.com
844-669-3957

ISBN: 978-1-6657-0001-6 (sc)
ISBN: 978-1-6657-0002-3 (e)

Library of Congress Control Number: 2020923879

Print information available on the last page.

Archway Publishing rev. date: 01/08/2021

DISCLAIMERS

The author has no vested or financial interests in any of the books herein mentioned. The mention of books has no commercial benefit to the author whatsoever. Specific books are only mentioned within the context of the themes of this text and for no other reason.

Recommendations of texts are simply that—recommendations. The reader should feel free to have in their own library or purchase whatever books they see fit for themselves.

My children's, grandchildren's, and various friends' names do not appear herein for the sake of privacy. They know who they are within the text. Persons who are mentioned by name are either deceased or have given written permission for their names to appear.

CONTENTS

THE BOOKS

For my family.

My greatest accomplishment in life has been
to help produce three good men.

If I have seen further, it is by standing on the shoulders of giants.
—Sir Isaac Newton

*A note on how to read this book: This writer uses many terms in this text. Some terms are in different languages, such as Hebrew and Yiddish. A glossary is provided at the end, to which the reader should refer, as well as references to the endnotes.

ACKNOWLEDGMENTS

I wish to thank my readers, my wife, Deborah Forman, my friend Nicholas Belmore, and the Archway staff for their help in preparing this manuscript for publication.

INTRODUCTION

My physician once asked me, "So, Stu, have you been a good man?" He was alluding the theological problem of whether I, having had so many serious life-threatening health challenges to face, deserved the good life I have. At the time of this writing, I am seventy-two years old, living with metastatic prostate cancer and having survived both lung cancer and aortic stenosis. I have a few things to say to my children, grandchildren, and anyone else who might be interested before I leave the world. And I want to answer my physician's question and challenge. So, this book is both a reflection and a legacy project. I have not found a good venue for such until this project.

As I wrote this work, I also felt that it might have some worth beyond my family. I do not pretend to be either wise or profound. But I have acquired a particular perspective on life. I hope that sharing it might be helpful to others as well.

This book is about my journey in life. It is also about my worldview. I have tried to intersperse the two in this text. As such, this work interweaves writing styles. Sometime it is engaging, and sometimes it can be academic. I hope the reader will bear with me. I am afraid that my oral communication is not much different.

In each chapter, I begin with one of the books that I determined to be formative for me. I do digress from the books in each chapter to also relate to the reader those life events that were happening during the time period in which I read those particular books. This is to hopefully put the texts within some contexts. I also provide some philosophical ideas that these books and time periods brought me to.

I think that waxing philosophical can, at times, be a form of melancholia. I am sure I have been melancholy for much of my life. Growing older and moving from a productive life into a far more constricted life can be a challenge. It is for me, and that is a part of the reason for writing this book. I want to be reflective about my life and learning.

I understand that suffering can be caused by attachments. I am not yet good enough at detachment. Like everyone, I have attachments. I am attached to a need to be valued. To wit, I feel the need to write about my life and my own strivings. Under the color of leaving a legacy project for my children and grandchildren, I recognize that such a project is also a means to hold onto ego. That being said, this is a part of who I am as a person. I cannot deny it, and, apparently, I am not a good enough Buddhist to detach from it, nor a good enough Taoist to just let it be as it is. Apparently, I am an old, neurotic Jewish guy learning to be an old, neurotic Jewish guy.

So, I acquiesced to ego and wrote this book about myself. What can I say? Everyone has strengths and failings. Both will be apparent herein. It is what it is …

The platform for this book began as an intellectual experiment that a close friend recommended to me. A few years ago, he told me of an exercise he had done to corral twelve books on a bookshelf representing those texts that had the most effect on his life. He thought this would be a good minimalist project to condense memories. He recommended the exercise to me.

I appreciated the idea and set off on this journey, which seemed to hold some promise in terms of identifying the important versus the superfluous. Unfortunately, probably because I am a verbose and somewhat obsessive person, I could not limit my books to twelve, no matter how hard I tried. I could get to thirty-seven books but no lower.

Now I should probably tell you that I have a rather complete library of hundreds of books. This is true even after purges through many housing moves. My library spans subjects from biology to philosophy to physics to economics to novels to reference texts to Judaica. I also collect antique books. I have been collecting books my entire life. So, this project was daunting.

I thought that once I settled on my thirty-seven texts, I would write an autobiography for my children and grandchildren, using these texts to illuminate my thoughts and how I arrived at them over my lifetime. I set out on that journey and was rather happy with myself about it. Then I spoke with my friend about it again.

This time, he told me that I did not do the exercise correctly and that he would not let me get away with having more than twelve books of important and formative texts on the shelf. He admonished me to go back and try harder. Some of this, he contended, was a rather Buddhist exercise in letting go, and some of it was condensing memories. That evening, I went back to the drawing board. In about an hour, I had paired down the list of thirty-seven to thirteen! I surprised myself. Well, it is a baker's dozen rather than just a dozen. What can I say?

Here are the thirty-seven books I originally selected out of my library, followed by the list of thirteen:

- *Wasp* by Eric Frank Russell (a science fiction built around the theme that one person can make a difference)
- *Anatomy and Physiology* (a book basic to medical science)
- *History of the World* by H. G. Wells
- *An Elementary Textbook of Psychoanalysis* by Charles Brenner, MD (a text that illuminates the science developed around unconscious determinism)
- *The Constitution of the United States* (politics and government)
- *Pirke Avot*, edited by Pinhas Kehati ("The Ethics of the Fathers" is a text on Jewish morality)
- *JB* by Archibald MacLeish(a play that is a modern presentation based on the theme of the book of Job or theodicy)
- *Catch-22*by Joseph Heller (a novel on the theme of the absurdity of war)
- *No Exit* by Sartre (an existential play)
- *The Myth of Sisyphus* by Albert Camus (an existential treatise)

- *Robert Frost* (a book of the poetry by this New England poet laureate)
- *Camping and Woodcraft* by Horace Kephart (outdoorsmanship)
- *The Absurd Healer* by Matthew P. Dumont, MD (a book on the theme of community psychiatry, not inconsistent with the theme of *Wasp*, the power to effect social change)
- *Ego and Instinct* by Peter Yankelovich and William Barrett (an update of psychoanalytic theory)
- *The True Believer* by Eric Hoffer (political philosophy regarding mass movements)
- *Tao Te Ching* by Lao Tzu (Oriental quietist philosophy)
- *Zen in the Martial Arts* by Joe Hyams (Zen as applied to the martial arts and to life)
- *Tao of Jeet Kune Do* by Bruce Lee (the philosophy and practice of martial arts)
- *Getting to Yes* by Fisher, Ury, and Patton (conflict management and negotiation)
- *Siddur Kol Yaakov* (an Orthodox Jewish prayer book and what I consider one of the, if not the most, important Jewish books)
- *A Brief History of Time: From the Big Bang to Black Holes* by Stephen Hawking (an introduction to physics)
- *Yosl Rakover Talks to God* by Zvi Kolitz (Holocaust and theodicy)
- *Anti-Semite and Jew* by Jean-Paul Sartre (anti-Semitism and prejudice)
- *On Apology* by Aaron Lazare, MD (self-explanatory title)
- *Words That Hurt, Words That Heal* by Rabbi Joseph Telushkin (the concept of evil speech in Judaism)
- *The Jewish Study Bible* by Adele Berlin and Marc Zvi Brettler (a text central to modern biblical study)
- *An End of Faith, Religion, Terror, and the Future of Reason* by Sam Harris (philosophy of religion)
- *Judaism Beyond God* by Rabbi Sherwin Wine (atheism and secular humanism in Judaism)
- *The Trial of God* by Elie Wiesel (the Holocaust and theodicy)

- *The Drunkard's Walk* by Leonard Mlodinow (a treatise on randomness)
- *The Grand Design* by Stephen Hawking and Leonard Mlodinow (physics)
- *The Origin of Species* by Charles Darwin (a treatise on evolution by natural selection)
- *The Blind Watchmaker* by Richard Dawkins (evolution)
- *God Is Everything* by Jay Michaelson (religion)
- *The Cave and the Light* by Arthur Herman (the foundations of Western philosophy through understanding Plato's and Aristotle's influences)
- *I Am Jewish* by Judah Pearl(Judaism, a testament to Daniel Pearl)
- *Why Be Jewish?* by Edgar Bronfman (secular Judaism)

The Baker's Dozen:

- *Wasp*
- *An Elementary Textbook of Psychoanalysis*
- *JB*
- *Catch-22*
- *The Tao Te Ching*
- *The Absurd Healer*
- *Zen in the Martial Arts*
- *Yosl Rakover Talks to God*
- *A Brief History of Time: From the Big Bang to Black Holes*[1]
- *Who Wrote the Bible*
- *Words That Hurt, Words That Heal*
- *An End of Faith, Religion, Terror, and the Future of Reason*[2]
- *The Drunkard's Walk—How Randomness Rules Our Lives*[3]

Even though I filtered my selection down to thirteen, each book is a segue into further study, and some of the books that we could segue to are very important in their own right. That is part of the reason why my first crack at this exercise ended with thirty-seven books. Some on that list are segued into by the thirteen and are referenced herein.

Seven decades is not a short time to talk about. There was a lot of reading, experiencing, thinking, and learning during my lifetime. There were themes that continued to play themselves out in my life. Getting to even a baker's dozen was very tough. But it still seemed incomplete. Something was missing.

As I reviewed the themes of my life and the literature that I attached to those themes, I kept finding phrases and aphorisms to be guides to important literature. For example, a section of dialogue I often quoted is from *JB*:

> If god is good, He is not god. If god is god, He is not good. Take the even, take the odd, I would not sleep here if I could, except for the little green leaves in the wood and the wind on the water.[4]

In finding the sources of phrases and aphorisms that have been in my repertoire of important thoughts, I found the literature that spawned these jewels and reduced them to the most important baker's dozen books that have helped to frame who I am and what I think about. That is what the project that my friend gave me was all about—pairing down memories and focusing only on the most important and formative things in my life. In doing the exercise, I also found that the borders of the empire of my memory were not always solid or complete. Memory can be like that … incomplete. You can forget sources, literature, and even people who gave you ideas to make into your own over time.

In exploring my college years for this project, I initially missed the influence of Kurt Vonnegut. It was not until I started to document and reference phrases in the process of due diligence to create this book that I found that I had done Mr. Vonnegut a deep disservice. Through some of the original number of cuts at creating the list of books that have been the most influential on me, I had forgotten exactly the power of certain phrases and concepts that Vonnegut's works had on me. I found this out through dealing with the phrase "chrono-synclastic infundibula."[5]

I located that phrase in memory in dealing with the importance of existentialism to me in my lifetime.

Memory often works through association. A word leads to a phrase, which leads to a series of thoughts and so forth. In trying to trace the literary sources of my existential thoughts (not the emotional sources), I knew how much *JB* and Archibald MacLeish had influenced me as a college freshman. In thinking about those early days of learning, I also related immediately to Joseph Heller's *Catch-22*. I knew how important Sartre and Camus were to me during college. I remember the importance that Samuel Beckett on my appreciating the theater of the absurd. But it was not until much later in the due diligence part of putting this work together that I realized how important Kurt Vonnegut's works have been in my life. Why did I forget them as the sources of various influential quotes and ideas? I use the phrase "I was a victim of a series of accidents, as are we all" all the time.[6] Why did Vonnegut not leap out at me in trying to put my literary list together?

Well, sometimes memory is like that. You just don't make the clear associations as an older person that you made as a younger one. So, in trying to reference the term "chrono-synclastic infundibula," I also realized that "I was a victim of a series of accidents, as are we all" came from *The Sirens of Titan*. And in finding that association in my memory, I also appreciated the power of Kurt Vonnegut to me in my lifetime! So, I could not keep my list to a baker's dozen anymore than I could have kept it to a dozen when I concluded that I could not leave out any of those thirteen books. *The Sirens of Titan* had to be included in my list, even if it made it longer. And so I included it. Explaining my life without it would have been incomplete at best and a personal scandal at worst!

So, with *The Sirens of Titan*, I finally settled on fourteen books in total to use in this writing project.

Why is all this even important?

There is a tradition among the Jewish people to write a Tzavah (a living ethical will) to your children and to give it to them before you pass. The purpose is to try to impart any wisdom you have acquired over life to help them improve their own lives. An ethical will can also produce discussion and intergenerational understanding. All of that seems laudable. There are many Jewish ethical wills over centuries preserved to examine.

I think that writing an autobiography based on the books that influenced me is almost like a Tzavah for my children. Sometime ago, they actually asked me to write them a Tzavah to explain how I, as an orthopraxis Jew, could also appreciate atheism. I spent a year composing that Tzavah. It did not particularly resonate with my children at that time. Perhaps this idea for a book will resonate. They understand my love of books and love of wisdom (the Greek words *philo*, or love, and *sophia*, or wisdom, define the word *philosophy*).

Wisdom is the accumulation of knowledge and the good sense to know what to do with it. One might not wish to presume to have wisdom until one is much older. I know some things. I have many regrets. One learns through both successes and failures. Much of what I have learned has been associated with text study. Obviously, I have also acquired understandings of life through experiences. And I was fortunate to have mentors who could help me integrate my experiences. Seventy-two is not a bad age at which to attempt such a project.

Texts have been my life. To explain who I am and how I got to be who I am through the medium of texts is an interesting endeavor. As the reader can see, my focus of attention includes answering some of life's big questions: What is the meaning of life? How does the universe work? What is the nature of being human? What does it mean to act ethically? What is the best way of being? What is the nature of absurdity? What does it mean to be a Jew? My quest has taken me into the deepest recesses of the human mind, into the quirkiness of physics, into the antiquity of the Bible, and into the wonders of mathematics.

Obviously, I am not done. I have been guided by a quote given to me years ago by a renowned Boston physician, "Learn as if you are to live forever. Live as if you are to die tomorrow." I was better at the first part than the latter, but I have always kept this quote before me. I hope that I keep learning the rest of whatever time life will allow me.

Who am I? This is a central question within this text. The theoretical physicist Carlo Rovelli has posited that "We are histories of ourselves, narratives."[7] This reflects thoughts of many other authors (physicists, psychologist, philosophers, poets, etc.) who have tried to answer this question of what is the nature of our self-conscious awareness. Rovelli adds to a long list of events that "I am what my reading has deposited in layers in my mind."[8] It seems appropriate, therefore, to set into context my own histories and narratives. I will do this by setting both a cultural and personal context within which the reader may evaluate those events and contexts that have framed my mind's answer to the question, "Who am I?"

BEGINNINGS:
AN ODE TO BOSTON
AND MASSACHUSETTS

I was born in Boston, Massachusetts, on November 20, 1947, at 2:30a.m. in the Boston Lying–In Hospital.

My family were immigrant Jews from Russia, both Litvak (maternally from the Baltic states) and Rushashuk (paternally from White Russia). My mother was born in Boston in 1917, and my father was born in Auburn, Maine, in 1915. Although a Jewish Russian second-generation American, my mother considered herself rather much of a Boston Brahmin. She was cultured and proud of being a Bostonian. She had been an English teacher and told me, "If you can't speak the King's English, don't speak!" Of course, by the time she said that to me, the king was dead, and there was a queen on the throne of England, but why quibble.

To be a Bostonian is to have a certain arrogance (sometimes conscious and sometimes not). Boston is known to itself as the "Hub of the Universe." It is a community that has some of the finest institutions of higher learning in the world and some of the greatest medical institutions. It is cultured and intelligent. Harvard University, Massachusetts Institute of Technology, Boston University, Boston College, Brandeis University, Wellesley College, Northeastern University, and so many other colleges and universities call metropolitan Boston and Massachusetts home. The Massachusetts General Hospital, Brigham and Women's Hospital, Dana

Farber Cancer Institute, the Boston Children's Hospital, Lahey Hospital and Medical Center, the Joslin Diabetes Center, the Deaconess-Beth Israel Hospital, the New England Baptist Hospital, and the McLean's Hospital are but a few of the world-renowned medical institutions in the Boston metropolitan area. World-class museums such as the Boston Museum of Fine Arts, the Elizabeth Stewart Gardener Museum, and the Peabody Museum of Natural History all call the metropolitan Boston area home. The Boston Pops, Boston Symphony Orchestra, and the Boston Philharmonic Orchestra bring music to the region. Students of music can study at the Berklee College of Music, the Longy School of Music, and the New England Conservatory of Music. The Boston Psychoanalytic Society is one of the oldest psychiatric associations in the US. The Massachusetts Medical Association (MMA) publishes the exceptional *New England Journal of Medicine* (NJM), and the Boston Medical Library (BML) is world-class. (I was extremely fortunate to have as a close colleague and friend the president of the MMA, the chief of the NJM, and the president of the BML, all in one personage.)

President John F. Kennedy was a Boston-born and bred politician. Tip O'Neill, former Speaker of the House of Representatives was the person who said, "All politics is local."Michael S. Dukakis served as governor of the commonwealth and became a Democratic nominee for the president of the United States.

The *Mayflower* landed in Plymouth, south of Boston, in 1620. Paul Revere took his famous midnight ride from Boston. George Washington defended Boston against the British from Dorchester Heights with cannons dragged from Ft. Ticonderoga in New York. Benjamin Franklin was born in Boston. The Boston Tea Party and the Boston Massacre both were important events that began our American Revolution. The "shot heard round the world" was fired at the Old North Bridge in Concord. The Shea's Rebellion of farmers began in Massachusetts. King Philip's War (or the *Red King's Rebellion* of the book by the same title) for freedom of native peoples began in southeastern Massachusetts and spread throughout New England in the seventeenth century. In the early 1800s, New Bedford, Massachusetts was one of the richest cities in

America based on whaling. Nantucket Island ran a close second, based on that industry. Herman Melville wrote *Moby Dick* with great reference to New Bedford whaling, and his pew remains at the Seamen's Bethel in that city. Henry David Thoreau wrote *Walden* about his experience at Walden Pond just west of Boston. The Massachusetts Fifty-Fourth was a regiment of African Americans led by white officers who distinguished themselves in the battle of Ft. Wagner during the Civil War. One of their surviving members won the Congressional Medal of Honor.

Boston is a sports town, being the home to the Boston Celtics, Boston Red Sox, the Boston Bruins, and the New England Patriots (based in Foxborough). Basketball was invented at Springfield College in Western Massachusetts. The Basketball Hall of Fame is located in Springfield, Massachusetts.

Who, born in Boston, would not be proud of the heritage of that city and the commonwealth?

To make matters *worse*, I am a product of the Newton Public School System, having attended Newton South High School. My elementary education began at the Mary Curley School in Boston (named after the wife of the famous Boston mayor Curley) before we moved to Newton in 1954 when I was in the second grade. Newton had, at that time, one of the best reputations for education in the country. Somewhat because of that education, I was able to graduate from the University of Massachusetts Amherst in three rather than four years, having received almost a semester's worth of advanced credits in German.

Humility in the face of this Massachusetts background is hard to obtain and maintain. Intellectual and cultural arrogance is easier to acquire than to rid one's self of. In fact, that aspect of a Bostonian's character might be generally unconscious for Bostonians. This is the coastal and northeastern stuff that the flyover nation despises and of which Bostonians are not fully aware as to how our geocentricism affects others. I am aware of this problem and still have trouble with my own Boston (and Massachusetts) geocentricism. I still consider myself a son of Massachusetts even though I now live in New York state. Anyone who listens to my pattern of speech knows I am a Bostonian.

My family was not just products of Boston and Massachusetts. Our family was Russian Jews and descendants of Eastern European Jewry who made their way to the US to escape poverty and persecution. According to Ancestry.com, I am genetically 100 percent Ashkenazi Jew. We could never be 100 percent Boston Brahmins. Boston has an informal caste system. Boston Brahmin status was reserved for wealthy WASPS (White Anglo-Saxon Protestants), and maybe for some Irish Catholics like the Kennedys, but not generally for Jews. The Jews had their own caste system. Stratifications are not uncommon in cultures.

Yet, even in being a Jewish person in Boston, there was cause for pride. The great Rav Joseph B. Soloveitchik taught at the Maimonides School in Brookline. Hebrew College, one of the regionally accredited independent schools of Jewish studies in the United States, is centered in Newton, Massachusetts (formerly Hebrew Teacher's College), and Brandeis University is located in Waltham, Massachusetts. It might not be New York City, but the Jewish communities in metropolitan Boston are no slouches either.

All of this is to say that one could easily come out of growing up in Boston and in Massachusetts with some sense of cultural superiority, intellectual arrogance, and geocentric loyalty. There was, during my growing up in Boston, also a strong sense of public service within Massachusetts as well.

President John F. Kennedy inspired my generation to be interested in public service. Senator Ted Kennedy's speech at the Democratic Convention, when he lost the nomination and said, "The work goes on, the dream still lives, and the hope shall never die," was more than a call to service. It was a call to hope. Hope is the greatest gift that humans have received from the universe. Hope has informed my work and my life. Growing up in Boston facilitated that too.

When Massachusetts opened the Bradford R. Burns Memorial PTSD Unit (for combat Vietnam veterans) at the Massachusetts Department of Public Health Rutland Heights Hospital (RHH) in 1987, I was asked to speak as the program's originator and director. I quoted Anne Frank's diary in my opening remarks when she wrote:

It's really a wonder that I haven't dropped all my ideals, because they seem so absurd and impossible to carry out. Yet, I keep them, because in spite of everything, I still believe people are good at heart. I simply can't build up my hopes on a foundation consisting of confusion misery and death. ... I think it will all come out right, and this cruelty too will end, and that peace and tranquility will return again. In the meantime, I must uphold my ideals for perhaps the time will come when I shall be able to carry them out.[9]

I became known to some of my combat Vietnam veteran patients as the "hope doctor."

Boston, for me, represents culture, intellectualism, scientific and medical achievement, and hope. Hope has been a theme of my life, informed by my experience, upbringing, environment, and, of course, reading. For me, intellectualism is not a dirty word. It is an accolade. And reading is a part of that.

So, this is the backdrop of my development. It is the canvas upon which my life evolved.

BEYOND GEOCENTRICISM

How does one get to where they are in life? What were the influences that produce one's efforts? The fourteen books that I picked are hoped to illuminate these questions as they pertain to my life. Along with the books themselves, I have discussed the events and times that existed when I read these texts in order to give context to my learning and understandings developed during those periods of my life. I am a firm believer that one cannot understand text without understanding its context. Nor can we understand a person without putting them into context. That is what I have tried to do herein.

In that sense, some personal additional recounting of my youth will set the stage to begin to examine the books.

I am an only child.

When I was born, my mother, father, Auntie Rae (my mother's sister), and I all lived together with my maternal grandparents at 35 Michigan Avenue in Dorchester, Massachusetts. Around the corner, at 107 Ellington Street, lived my father's parents. Up the street, down the street, across the street, and all around our immediate residence, people were Jewish. People were generally new immigrants, first and second generation. People spoke "Yinglish" or a mixture of Yiddish and English. Many, if not most of the men my father's age had served in WWII, which had ended only two years before. It was very much a shtetl form of community. It was close-knit in businesses, culture, and at home. It felt safe because of its uniformity.

Boston was somewhat primitive in the late 1940s and early 1950s. We heated our apartment with kerosene, which sat in a big jug on top of the stove. The stove was used for heat as well as for cooking. I remember the ice man, the rag man, the man who came with a grinding wheel to sharpen knives, and the pot man selling pots. Everyone was trying to make a living peddling whatever they could.

I remember going with my grandmother to buy herring at a store in a basement with barrels of herring and pickles that the seller wrapped in newspaper for us. There was sawdust on the floor. I remember the smell. I remember the seller and my grandmother spoke Yiddish. My grandmother would make pickled herring. It was not unlike Eastern Europe in many of those respects.

When I was three years old in 1950, I had plastic surgery on my ears at the Boston Children's Hospital. My ears had grown to look like little cuppy chimpanzee ears. I saw the pictures taken before surgery, and they saddened me. I looked like Dumbo.

The operation was a new one. My parents fretted about the results. I was separated from my parents for at least a week. They were not allowed to visit until I was recovered enough. I do not know who was more traumatically affected by this antiquated hospital policy, me or my parents.

Instead of my parents visiting, my pediatrician, Harry Shwachman, MD, visited me. His office and laboratory were at Boston Children's Hospital. He was a great research scientist in the field of cystic fibrosis and a good friend of our family. His son and I have been best of friends since childhood. I did not have cystic fibrosis, but I was fortunate to have Dr. Shwachman as my pediatrician because of our family's relationship. Harry became the archetype for me of the noble physician. I tried to model myself after his example of diligence and compassion. He was my doctor, my mentor, and our family friend.

For a year after the operation, I had to wear a helmet so as not to damage the ears. My father, in particular, was so overprotective of my ears that he would not let barbers fold my ears forward to cut the hair around them. I was not allowed to play outside with other kids unless in was gentle play in the sandbox or supervised by my parents. This overprotection lasted for years after my surgery. It took me a long time to be able to go to a barbershop without worrying that my ears might come off.

In fact, when we had children, the first thing my father did was examine their ears … not their sex or whether they had five fingers and toes on each hand and foot. No, he examined their ears. He had been traumatized by my genetic deformity.

My mother and me in 1951. I am wearing my ear helmet.

This sense of being different had a negative effect. I adopted the anxiety of my parents. It probably affected my desire to play team and contact sports. These experiences did not stop me from being a social character. I did adopt the idea of my fragility from my parents though. I was always a slight little kid, so my sense of being fragile was easy to reinforce. I relied, instead, on my personality and intellect.

It would not be too much to say that my plastic surgery at age three was a major life trauma and left an indelible psychic scar. Additionally, in those days, surgery was done under ether. I can remember the cup being placed over my nose in the operating theatre, and I felt like I was drowning. I am sure this had a long-term effect on my ability to swim with my face in the water or even to have water in my face when getting a shampoo.

During the summers, we vacationed in Onset, Massachusetts, "down the Cape" (Cape Cod). We rented a cottage in a Jewish area. It was not indigenously Jewish, but it was a summer vacation spot for Jews on Cape Cod. There were many Orthodox people in the area we stayed in. Sometimes that caused friction because we were not Orthodox and did not keep strictly kosher. But, like Dorchester and Newton, Onset in the summer felt Jewish nonetheless. It was a mini-shtetl.

We were there in 1954 for Hurricane Carol. This was traumatic as well because we were evacuated by the National Guard to dry, higher land. My father was working in Boston when the hurricane struck. He drove down from Boston after the hurricane, and he and I walked the beach. Boats had been tossed everywhere. Houses had crashed on the shore. Sheep were dead along the shoreline. There were National Guard soldiers with machine guns guarding the destroyed boats. It was devastating and frightening. I learned that you can't fool with Mother Nature.

Me on Onset Beach after Hurricane Carol in 1954

Vulnerability was an issue within my young development. Whether it was vulnerability due to illness or to physical size or to understanding that we had little control over nature, or even meeting my father's expectations … vulnerability was an issue in my young life.

Vulnerability was one of the sequelae of trauma for my grandparents as well. My paternal step-grandmother had lost her family (husband and two children) in a pogrom and slept with packed bags for the rest of her life, lest she would have to leave quickly. Both of my grandmothers had survived pogroms. I can only assume that my grandfathers did too. Such behavior affected my father as well. It has been multi-generationally handed on to me.

We moved to Newton, Massachusetts, in 1954 as a part of what became known as the "white flight" from Boston. It was a standard migration for upwardly mobile Jews to move out of Dorchester and Mattapan to the suburbs of Brookline and Newton. Those communities became predominantly Jewish, while our neighborhoods in Dorchester and Mattapan became predominantly black and poor. This was all encouraged by banks redlining during the 1950s. It was a shameful era for integration. It inadvertently contributed to keeping the Jewish community intact.

The section of Newton we moved to was essentially split between two ethnic groups, Italians and Jews. The only anti-Semitism I ever ran into as a youngster was an offhand comment by an Italian neighbor and some kids on the street who called a group of us "dirty kikes." Other than that, anti-Semitism was relatively absent in my world until I got to college. Much like other ethnic groups, Jews tended to cluster together. They built large synagogues (testaments to their economic success), established Hebrew schools, and ran businesses. There were kosher markets and delicatessens. Newton was no longer a shtetl like Dorchester had been, because of its wealth. But it might just as well have been one.

Just like in Dorchester, most people I knew and associated with were Jewish. Christians and Jews intermingled. But my friendship patterns and world experiences were very much predominantly Jewish.

Newton itself had a high percentage of Jews in the population. There were other Christian ethnic groups. I learned to navigate those because of my girlfriend and other non-Jewish friends I had made. There was a whole WASP society that I became familiar with through friends. Where we lived, there were both Jews and Italians. They were all always kind to me. I never felt like "the Jewish kid." But I was always on guard. I had internalized Jewish paranoia from my grandparents and parents.

Being Jewish became a major self-identification. My parents made sure that I went to a Conservative-Orthodox ("Conservadox") Hebrew school, which influenced me a lot. My Hebrew school teachers were mentors to me. My bar mitzvah teacher and his family gave me a view of Orthodox life that I appreciated and identified with.

When we lived in Jamaica Plain, my father sponsored a hero Israeli soldier of the 1948 War of Independence to come to study in the US. My father made sure that I knew of this man's exploits and that I honored his Jewish military service in the Israeli Defense Forces. Being Israeli was something to look up to … up until I considered Aliyah (moving to Israel). Then it was no good from my father's perspective.

Even though we did not keep kosher, my mother would not think of buying meat anywhere but the Jewish butcher in Newton Centre. There was a certain conflict within our family between observance and nonobservance. It was as if my parents valued Orthodoxy but rejected it at the same time. They always had conflict with how *Jewish* I was and was becoming. My father played golf every Shabbat, while I often went to shul (junior high into high school). It left me in conflict as well.

In Newton, our house backed up to a large playground attached to Bowen Elementary School. My father, an avid golfer with a four handicap, was often in the playground practicing his swing. I had my first little golf club when we lived in Jamaica Plain (after leaving living with my maternal grandparents in 1950). My father would take me to run around after him at the Franklin Park Golf Course in Boston. When we moved to Newton and had a long playground in which to hit golf balls, my father determined that it was time for me to actually learn how to play golf. I was seven years old when this activity began.

He would take me out back into the playground to teach me golf. Golf was his passion, and he was obsessive about it. He really wanted me to perform for him. But he was not a good teacher. He was overly perfectionistic. When my performance did not meet his standards, I was derided with foul names. I felt this as fairly traumatic. I never understood why my father was so angry with me. As I reflect upon this, he was not angry with me. He was angry at me because I was a reflection of himself in his own mind. But his verbal degradations followed me my entire life.

This verbal abuse was present in most areas of my life. As a little boy, if I made a mistake and brought my father a wrench rather than a pair of pliers, I would be derided. If I brought home a bad mark from school, watch out. He would do spelling tests with me, and if I made a mistake, I was called derisive names. I began to get rather much of an inferiority complex and secluded myself in my room often. My mother and her sister who lived with us (Auntie Rae) were ineffective in intervening. I developed a sense that I could not do anything right. That had a lifelong negative effect. I loved my father, but I just wanted to be distanced from the verbal degradation.

My mother, aunt, and maternal grandmother (Nana) tried to compensate for the rough environment in the house that my father generated. They were people who showed me unconditional positive regard and love. They felt I was special and would come to do great things in my life. I tried to listen to that message but also incorporated the message from my father ... *I did not meet his expectations and was a deficient person.*

Still, I was given advantages by my parents and by Auntie Rae. I got to play a series of instruments, beginning with piano, then clarinet, then classical guitar. This was all under the influence of my classical pianist mother. We had a baby grand piano in the house to practice on.

My mother had learned the piano in Boston. She used to tell the story that when they moved to Ft. McClellan, Alabama, with the army during WWII, she worked in a music store because of her ability to play the piano. The customers did not want to hear her play classical music, however. They wanted "Onward Christian Soldiers," which my mother learned to play for customers at the music store.

Auntie Rae frequently took me to the Boston Museum of Fine Arts. One of my father's friends took me to "rush" symphony and the Boston Pops on Friday nights. I spent time in the cryogenics lab at MIT where my aunt worked as administrative assistant (for thirty-six years). I learned to skate at the Lars Anderson Estate. I studied equestrian dressage. I had many exposures and advantages.

My father was born in Auburn, Maine, and felt that a young man should have rural interests, such as how to fish, shoot, survive in the woods, ride horses, and canoe. He used to go fishing with a large group of male friends twice a year in Forest City, New Brunswick (town of fifty persons between the American side and the Canadian side). He started taking me when I was ten in 1957. In later life, I took each of my boys when they turned ten to the same spot with the same guide.

Because of my father's perfectionism, he left my learning of fly-fishing to his good friends. Louie taught me how to fly-fish, and our guides taught me how to canoe, use a knife and ax, and start a fire in the woods. My father's friends relieved me from his teaching. Everyone knew how hard he was on me and that it was best for me to learn from others. I was not as aware of that as a youngster as I was when I got older.

But when my father got intoxicated (a pastime in the woods of Canada for this group), he became quite mellow. All the harshness ceased. Only then did I feel at ease with him. After he died, I continued those trips. To this day, I have a picture of Forest City in my house, reminding me of those times of bonding with adult men. I was the only youngster on those trips. The wilderness and male bonding were a great source of comfort to me throughout my life. Forest City was one place where I felt close to my father.

One year, on one of my trips in the 1980s after my father passed away, my guide came to tell me that the owner of the camp on the stream where we often fished had decided that he did not want fishermen disturbing his privacy in this remote location. That was a sentimental site for me, being the first camp that my father took me to. The camp owner made one exception, however. He would let me fish in front of his camp anytime I wished. Why was such a privilege extended to me? I questioned. "Well," said my guide, "we all saw how rough you father was on you, and we felt badly for you. You can fish there any time you want to."

Fishing "The Stream" in New Brunswick, Canada

I felt embarrassed and devastated for myself and embarrassed for my father. I never fished in front of that camp again.

The first camp I went to with my father in Canada in 1957.

On the trips to Forest City after my father's passing, it took a couple of years for my guide to stop calling me "Al." Was I that much like my father? I wondered. It was an honor to be thought of as others thought of him because everyone knew him as an extremely generous and ethical person. But I was not Al. No one but Al could be Al.

Despite these conflicts, my father was probably the most important person in my life. He was highly respected in business. He was a very ethical and generous person. I hoped that I had acquired those traits and not the traits of harshness (that only a few people saw).

But I knew the darker side that others did not. Well, some people in Forest City saw some of it, as the story above shows. But most people thought that to be Al's son was an honor and a blessing. You can't fly too close to a bright flame unless you want to get burned. It is generally easier to be a person's friend than his son.

As my father's representative in the world, I felt an obligation to live up to his good qualities and to protect his name. I do not know how well I have done. I have a lot of him in me. Just telling these stories raises some conflicted feelings. But they are truths that have made me who I am.

Sundays were rifle range day. My two good friends Geoff Belinfante and another lifelong friend (we three and our families have remained close friends to this day) used to come with us. My father taught us how to shoot pistols, rifles, and shotguns. I got my first BB gun at eleven and my first .22 rifle when I was thirteen. I was allowed to keep the firearm and ammo in my room. Times were indeed different then. It was a great sense of trust that was placed in me.

My mother and aunt never complained about guns in the house. My father kept a loaded .22 Smith and Wesson Model 18 revolver in his nightstand. He told me not to touch it, and I did not. This was one of the few areas in which I excelled over my father's expectations. I was a good shot.I was respectful and safe with firearms. I was never without a gun again until I was sixty-five years old. Guns were a bond to my father. It took quite a bit for me to give up gun ownership in deference to my wife's requests in later life.

I even took my rifle to college in 1965 and shot at the ROTC range. I remember the first night in my dormitory when our "dorm ma'am" (who everybody called "Ma") gathered us all together and said, "Okay, boys, hand over your guns. I'll lock them up, and you can have them when you need them." You can't believe the armament that came out of the woodwork! It was 1965, and the 1968 Federal Gun Control Act had not yet been passed. Today, you certainly cannot have a gun on campus unless you want to go to prison. Times were different.

My father told me that a gentleman was never without a handkerchief, a wallet, and a pocketknife. That has been and still is my "EDC" or "everyday carry." My maternal grandfather gave me my first pocketknife when I was eleven years old. I carried it everywhere, even to junior high school. I still own that little knife. Life was different back then in so many ways. People did not think about guns and knives as we do today because of our society's misuse of them. My exposure to guns and knives had a rather rural context, stemming from my Maine-born father, even though we lived in the suburbs of Boston.

By the way, such an upbringing with Maine rural values was antithetical to a Jewish upbringing of intellectualism. Fishing, woodscraft, and shooting were not generally within the scope of concern of my Jewish friends. Those things were within the scope of understanding of my few Christian friends, however. To that degree, I was somewhat conversant in two different worlds and a Jewish anachronism and iconoclast.

This was the world of my youth and some issues that set the stage for how I understood the world. The themes of my developmental young life included a sense of vulnerability and a sense of personal inadequacy. I maintained the hope that I could somehow meet my father's expectations. I was buoyed up by the strength of the important women in my life (my mother, her sister, and my maternal grandmother) and the most important person in my life, my maternal grandfather.

I also developed a good chunk of Jewish paranoia from my parents and grandparents. That, too, has lasted throughout my life.

So, the stage is set. Here we go with the fourteen books that I attribute to having been formative to my personal history, thoughts and character and the events of my life.

The Books

*A note to the reader: After each section begun by the title of a book, there is a date that follows. That is not the date of publication but rather the date at which I read that particular book.

Wasp by Eric Frank Russell, Read in 1958

> Compared to a human being, the wasp's size is minute,
> its strength negligible. ... Nevertheless, that wasp killed
> four big men and converted a large powerful car into a
> heap of scrap.[10]

It was interesting to me that the first real book that I read and appreciated as influential on my life was science fiction called *Wasp* by Eric Frank Russell. I have no real memory of how I came to this book. I do wish that I could remember, but it was a long time ago. I was about eleven years old.

I tried to retrieve the memory of how I came to this book by running the matter by my good friend Geoffrey Belinfante, who I have known since I was seven years old. He actually remembered reading the book too but not how we both came to it as kids. Neither of us could remember. If anyone might have known, it would have been my friend Geoff.

We have been friends since second grade. Our mothers were the best of friends and loved each other. We had numerous similar experiences growing up together, as we were both only children. We went to the same schools and had many of the same friends, even to this day. He was my best man at my first wedding, and I scribed his wife's Ketubah (Jewish marriage contract, which is the property of the wife).Our families went camping together every summer. Forty-two years later, my son married his daughter, and I scribed her Ketubah as I had done for her mother forty-two years earlier. We have two grandsons in common. Quite a story!

I have been very blessed in my life by long-term relationships such as the one I just mentioned. I have close friends from elementary school, junior high, high school, college, the service, graduate school, and employments. My college roommate, Ed Toomey, was best man at my second marriage, and I was his best man at his wedding. We remain close to this day.

In any event, sometimes people can help me remember things I have lost to the province of memory. But since most of us are now older, turning to friends to fill in memory gaps does not always work.

Oh well. I do remember *Wasp* and its contents. I should be happy with that. I have a copy of the book in my library.

The book's theme unfolds itself through the venue of a war. But its real theme is about disruption, societal change, and the power of a single individual to effect change. Something as small as a wasp could destroy a car and all of its occupants. That theme and happening is revealed early on in the book; a wasp flies into a car with four occupants who begin to swat at the wasp. This causes a loss of control of the car by the driver, which winds up killing all of the occupants. That theme has directed me and stuck with me my entire life—*something seemingly small can affect something much larger.* Never underestimate the power of a single individual to do either good or bad. In fact, never underestimate the power of a single individual.

Wasp was written in 1957, and I read it shortly after that date. I was a latency-age kid, but its theme affected me. As a Bostonian Jew, I had a sense of commitment to community and to public service, already inculcated in me even then. *Wasp* encouraged me that even little me could make a difference. It gave me encouragement and hope. It reinforced the messaging from my mother, her sister, and their mother and father. That is why *Wasp* holds a place as first of the fourteen books that I chose as formative for me and my life direction.

It is unfortunate, of course, that one must learn about societal change through the venue of war. But that is what sells science fiction books, I guess.

Anyway, the idea that a tiny entity, a single person, could create large change was impressive to a latency-old Jewish kid who was anxious and not very sure of himself. It encouraged me. Maybe even I, the person who never seemed to be able to do anything right, who developed sensitivity and a poor self-image of some personal inadequacy, could have a social impact and do good for people. And if I could effect change for others, perhaps I could help others who were suffering, as I was, to feel better. And in some roundabout way, perhaps that could help me to feel more enfranchised and feel better too. It was a stage setter for my personal and professional life. It helped sublimate my demons into a life of social justice and fairness.

I did not then, and do not now, like suffering. I don't like it for me, and I do not like it for others. I do not like it for human beings, and I equally do not like it for animals (our fellow travelers in life). Maybe that is why Buddhism seemed so appealing to me in later life. The central core of Buddhism is the relief of suffering.

In my original list, you may note that *Wasp* did not take the honorable place of first in my books. That originally went to the book *Anatomy and Physiology*. I had originally selected this book because it was given to me by my favorite Hebrew school teacher on the occasion of my bar mitzvah in 1960. That book interested me because of my idea to become a physician, as my father wanted me to. But really, on reflection, I chose the book because of my teacher's most encouraging inscription in that book.

My family at my bar mitzvah in 1960. Left to right:
Grandparents Harry ("Hipop") and Ida ("Nana") Levin, Mother
Jeanette (Levin) Forman, me, Father Isaac (Al) Forman, and
Rachel P. Levin ("Auntie Rae"). My paternal grandfather had
already passed, and my grandmother was very ill at the time.

Everyone needs mentors (certainly I did). My parents were mentors, my aunt was a mentor, my physician was a mentor, my bar mitzvah tutor was a mentor, and my sixth-grade Hebrew school teacher was a mentor to me. He had faith in me when I did not have faith in myself. His inscription letter in the book he gave me for my bar mitzvah buoyed me up at the time and encouraged me to look ahead to do great things and "to see further."[11] That is also why I delimited it from my list of thirty-seven. You cannot choose a book for its inscription. It should be chosen for its content.

However, since many of the thirty-some-odd books that I originally chose are still really of significance, I set up the bookshelf of important books with the fourteen leading the way and the rest of the originally chosen books rounding out the entire bookshelf. I still read my teacher's letter to me in *Anatomy and Physiology* when I need encouragement. It gave, and still gives me, hope. Hope is a theme in my life.

I should not overlook the fact that the book that I first considered choosing was a book of science. The formulation of my interest in the sciences began quite early. My maternal (auntie) Rae Levin was administrative assistant in the Department of Cryogenic Engineering at MIT for thirty-six years. Because of her, some of my youth was spent in that laboratory, including working there the summer before college. Exposure to MIT scientists helped form my interest in and appreciation of science and the scientific method. *Anatomy and Physiology* was my original choice of a formative text for all of these reasons.

Upon reflection, stimulated by my friend who gave me this book project, it was really *Wasp* that was the most and originally formative book I read even before I read *Anatomy and Physiology*. I am glad that my first book was science fiction and not a medical textbook. It makes me feel more normal. What latency-old kid would choose a medical textbook as one of their most influential books anyway?

The idea of social change, of being a change agent, of being able to affect larger systems for the benefit of people directed my life's work. It was a concept that invigorated and empowered my thoughts about myself. Sometimes I did not realize how influential *Wasp* was on me. But it was most certainly influential.

Wasp is a book that gives permission and enfranchisement to the individual. Even though I did not have great faith in myself as a young man, I did somehow have a strong sense of leadership and was committed to improving the world. My father was charismatic within his circle of friends and business associates, and my mother had absolute confidence in me. Both strands of self-conceptualization existed simultaneously within me. Understanding that I could make a difference was important, and it is interesting that this came to me, in part, through a science fiction book. I really was a science fiction buff right into college.

Of course, in college, one had to read science fiction such as Robert Heinlein's *Stranger in a Strange Land* as well Tolkien's *Hobbit* and trilogy. And who could forget *The Sirens of Titan* and *Slaughterhouse Five* by

Kurt Vonnegut? I devoured all of these science fiction books. Somehow, after college, my interest in science fiction began to wane. Today, I barely read such things at all, having defaulted to physics, theology, and philosophy. Life changes things as one ages through its journey. The exigencies of life take over, and the best of plans and interests can become diverted. As John Lennon said, "Life is what happens while you are making other plans."

So, in summary, what did I learn from *Wasp*? *I learned the power of an individual to effect change.* That learning would help determine my life course.

An Elementary Textbook of Psychoanalysis
by Charles Brenner, MD, 1964

So much of what goes on in our minds is unconscious.[12]

Education, science, medicine, culture, service, and Judaism were all themes that evolved throughout my youth, supported by my family, my religion, and my culture.

I was not the best student though. I did get a double promotion in math in sixth grade, but that did not help me once I reached junior high. I did not grasp math concepts well in high school either. I was doing so well at math in elementary school. Too bad for me that this skill did not seem to continue. This was also very unfortunate for me, as the fields that I was interested in required a lot of math. If I ever get to come back (I do not believe in reincarnation), I hope that I will be better at math in a next life.

I did win first- and second-place awards in science fairs in junior high and an honorable mention from the National Academy of Science in seventh grade (1960). So, it was not that I was not a good science student. I just wasn't an outstanding classroom student overall. I was a good scientist outside the classroom and in laboratory but not a good mathematician.

I had and continue to have a great love of history and English. I excelled at these subjects probably because my father had once been a history teacher and my mother an English teacher. But my concentration in the classroom was not what it should have been in my younger years and, indeed, into college. I did not academically excel until I reached graduate school. In my first master's program I graduated with a straight 4.0 GPA! That made up for my rather tepid undergraduate performance.

I was always much better at conceptualization than at formulas. I was also good at interpersonal relationships and leadership. I was able to manage conflict and often befriended less fortunate and/or delinquent students when others had little to do with them. These skills in conflict management came from managing my father's anger and the parental conflicts in the family home.

My father was not one to express love directly. In fact, just the opposite; he was difficult to manage and rough on my mother, my aunt, and myself. Years later, I found letters from his brother to him during WWII that illuminated that he was difficult even in his youth and that he took out his frustrations on the people closest to him. His adjustment to the army took some doing, as his brother seemed to comment in his letters. My father was never good at being told what to do. My sons and I are that way too. We either have to be in charge or work for someone we really respect to be well adjusted in the working world. It is a case of multigenerational transmission.

My father lost his mother when he was eight months old. My biological grandmother, Sara (Smith) Forman, died of endocarditis in 1916 in Auburn, Maine. My two-times paternal great-uncle Joe had emigrated with my paternal great-aunt Fanny (his niece) from Russia to Worcester, Massachusetts. They later brought my grandfather, Harry (Gershon) Forman, to the USA. Their father, Yitzak Forman, had died from rabies at age forty in Russia. As the family story goes, my great-great-uncle Joe got into financial trouble in Worcester and "escaped" with his nephew, my paternal grandfather, Harry, to Maine. His niece (my great-aunt Fanny Forman Margolis) married in Worcester and remained there with her family.

In Maine, my great-great-uncle and his nephew married two sisters in the same Smith family. My biological grandmother, Sara (Smith)

Forman, died at twenty-six years old in 1916, eight months after giving birth to my father. My father was nursed by his maternal aunt Goldie, along with her own son, until my grandfather married (an arranged marriage) Fanny Ashmon, also from Russia. Fanny had lost her family in a pogrom in Russia and had come to the United States.

Harry and Fanny had two children together, Morris and Hyman. We never spoke of my uncles as "step" family members. We never mentioned Sara in my family until my father passed away in 1980. The familial attempt, I believe, was to be one family and not have half-family members. All this came as a great shock to my Forman first cousins when they discovered the matter of our grandfather's first marriage.

My father himself believed that he was treated differently by his stepmother versus her own children. Whether that was truth or perception on his part, we will never know. His own father was fairly emotionally aloof. My grandfather made the best home he could with his new wife and children. He worked in a shoe factory and got pulmonary illness from the toxic fumes there. I never knew him when he was not sick. In his younger days, he had the reputation of being a very strong man who could legendarily lift up the front of cars and unbend horseshoes.

It is a hell of a thing to lose your mother so early and to be brought up by a stepmother with a sick and aloof father. I had empathy for my father's sufferings in these regards.

My father went to work early to help support the family. He supported the family his entire life. I have his shoe-shining kit that he used on the streets of Boston when he was very young. He shined shoes for a couple of cents, and the money went to the family. In later life, he had to quit his college studies to go to work to help the family financially. His dreams of becoming a physician were not realized, and he was hurt by that. Perhaps his over expectations for me were somewhat based on this family story.

My father took care of his stepmother as if she were his biological mother and assisted his stepbrothers throughout their lives as if they were his full biological brothers. He said Kaddish three times a day for eleven months for Bubby Fanny, as prescribed by Jewish law. One of the

only things he ever asked me to do for him was to care for his biological
mother's grave in Maine after he would die.

Whenever we went to Canada fishing, we would always stop at his
mother's grave in Auburn, Maine, to say the memorial prayer, "El Moley
Rachamim" ("God, full of compassion"). The year before he died, we
were at the grave, and he grabbed my hand and said, "Don't let my
mother's grave fall into disrepair after I'm gone."

"Okay," I said.

"I mean it!" he said emphatically.

"I promise," I assured him. He died the following year, 1980, of a
massive coronary at age sixty-five. Most of us believed that he must have
known that he was ill at that time but did not want to admit it. I was
thirty-three years old. He missed everything.

My father's anger somehow always hearkened back to the early loss
of his mother, Sara. This did not excuse his verbal abuse of those closest
to him, but it did make it more understandable.[13] Despite these early
losses, my dad grew up to be a charismatic and very ethical person. He
was liked by all who knew him. It was just tough to be his son.

Bowenian family systems theory recommends understanding one's
parents as someone else's children. It is easier to differentiate yourself
as an individual when you understand your parents as individuals.
That was something I really tried to do. That is why I was attracted to
psychoanalysis. It really did help me to understand and have compassion
for my father and for the unconscious forces that framed his behavior.

The fact that I knew the origins of my father's behaviors intuitively
pointed me in the direction of becoming a psychologist. Of course,
being Jewish, growing up in Newton, and coming from Boston, my
first thoughts were to become a psychiatrist. But I would never have the
marks in college to attend medical school, much to my father's chagrin.
He had wished to become a physician and served as a medic in WWII.
He never had the money and had to quit Boston University as a young
person to help support the family. So he wished that his son would
complete his vision and become a physician. I had tried to orient my

future to those anticipations. I should have tried to please myself and not my father's expectations.

In 1964, I discovered a book for sale in the library at Newton South High School (NSHS). It was *An Elementary Textbook of Psychoanalysis* by Charles Brenner, MD. It cost ninety-five cents. I spent an inordinate time considering whether or not to buy this book and part with the ninety-five cents. Finally, with the encouragement of my high school girlfriend (we would later marry after college and then divorce three and a half years later), I did buy the book. Thus began my career toward becoming a psychologist. In fact, I think that *An Elementary Textbook of Psychoanalysis* may be one of the most important books in my entire library.

Now, becoming a psychologist, or even a psychiatrist, was not my father's vision of becoming a "real physician." In fact, when I told him that psychology was the profession I wanted to pursue, he wept. He just did not feel that I could make a living in that kind of profession. He made me agree that I would take the premedical curriculum in college, even if I majored in psychology. He wanted me to fulfill his dream to become a doctor. He probably was not happy that I had Charles Brenner's little book on psychoanalysis.

In college, I minored in philosophy and loved it. One day, I told my father that I might like to teach philosophy. He was not pleased by that either. It took me another forty-seven years to become an adjunct college faculty teaching philosophy. I taught a lot of philosophy courses; Introduction to Philosophy, Ethics, the Art of Reasoning, Philosophy of Science, and Major World Religions. I often wonder if my father would have been proud of that or not.

My mother knew about Freud and was not impressed by his sexual theories. The only person in the house whom I could discuss Charles Brenner's book with was Auntie Rae. She lived with us for as long as I can remember. When we moved from living with my maternal grandparents in Dorchester to Jamaica Plain, Auntie Rae came with us to escape her parents. In fact, when my parents moved to Aniston, Alabama, during

WWII, Auntie Rae joined them there. She lived with us my entire young life until after my father passed away.

My parents' relationship was no less conflicted than their parents' relationships. In multigenerational Bowenian theory, people tend to replicate the family of origin in their own lives to try to solve the conflicts in their own generation. People often marry people who represent the conflicted parent in the family or origin. My mother, in that sense, married her mother, with whom she was conflicted.

My maternal grandmother was as tough as my father. She was very stubborn and difficult to manage. She was very loving and generous but also very difficult. My grandfather used to get so aggravated by her that he had fainting spells after their arguments, according to my mother and my aunt. My mother and her sister never had a great relationship with their own mother because of that conflict. Both sisters were devoted to their father. To a degree, in the structure of my nuclear family, my mother took on the role of her father, and my father represented her mother in the multigenerational transmission of intra-familial conflict.

The real issue in families is to differentiate where you begin and end versus where your parents' egos exist. Differentiation of self can be a *striving* within a lifetime pursuit of defining oneself. My aunt defined herself by moving to Florida to be independent after my father passed.

Now Auntie Rae was a bit of a fruitcake, but she kept my head together as a kid. She read *Mad* magazine with me surreptitiously in her room at home. If my father had known that we had *Mad* magazine in the house, there would have been hell to pay. So too with Charles Brenner's book on psychoanalysis, I think. But to Auntie Rae, it was all okay. After all, her world was at MIT. Science (if one could call psychoanalysis a science) and medicine were fully within her scope of appreciation. And so I first discussed Freud and the unconscious with my aunt.

In the study of the mind according to psychoanalytic theory, I discovered the role that the unconscious plays in determining behavior, the structure of the psychic apparatus, and the role of the defense mechanisms. I learned about the development of anxiety and of mental illnesses. I discovered the maturation process and the role of sexuality and aggression.

I began reading Freud's works, facilitated by my courses in German in junior high and high school. By the time I went to college, I was fluent in German, and this aided not only my psychology studies but my science studies. All of this psychoanalysis I acquired by myself. I even began to interpret my own dreams, writing them down upon awakening each day. By the time I went to college at age seventeen, I had read not only Charles Brenner's book but also Freud's *The Interpretation of Dreams, Future of an Illusion, The Ego and the Id, Civilization and Its Discontents, Moses and Monotheism,* and *Three Essays on the Theory of Sexuality.* I read Carl Jung's *Man and His Symbols* and *An Outline of Psychoanalysis,* edited by Thompson, Mazer, and Wittenberg. This entire course of investigation and study began with Charles Brenner and his little book.

In high school, I was able to take a course in psychology. We studied Eric Fromm's book *The Art of Loving.* It was not rigorous enough for me. Through Brenner's book, I came to appreciate the unconscious and unconscious determinism. Anything else seemed like metaphysics, and I already did not like metaphysics. It was not testable or provable. Then again, neither was psychoanalysis! But who among my teachers was there to discuss psychoanalysis with in high school? No one. Our psychology teacher was interested in humanistic forms of psychology, not psychoanalysis. So I had to teach myself about the unconscious, unconscious determinism, the structure of the psychic apparatus, and its defense mechanisms. That was a lot for a sixteen- or seventeen-year-old kid to attempt on his own.

Understanding that there is unconscious determinism was a huge piece of awareness for me. The fact that I recognized that my father's anger dated back to the loss of his mother meant to me that I already had an intuitive sense about the workings of the mind. Yet all of this lay dormant until after college. That is because the psychology department at the University of Massachusetts Amherst was a behaviorally oriented psychology department and had little or nothing to offer me in terms of psychodynamics at an undergraduate level.

I graduated high school at age seventeen in 1965.

During my high school years, I underwent a form of transformation of thought and values that would last me my entire life. It was, of course, the sixties. Vietnam was cranking up. There was a sexual revolution going on. Civil rights and the feminist movement were happening. Folk music was becoming the marketplace for ideas and revolution. Socialism was in the air. The classical guitar I had been studying began to give way to folk music.

I studied classical guitar. Once a week, I would troop into the Steiner Building in Boston for my lessons. The building was the home to many music teachers of various instruments and operatic voice training. Music would waif out of every office in that building. It was lovely and emotionally stimulating.

Classical guitar and classical music are very demanding and, I feel, gave me a certain discipline and sense of organization that helped me all my life. I wrote and composed music. My turn to folk music represented a loosening of that discipline, so representative of the 1960s.

Despite the fact that I studied classical guitar, composed music, and taught guitar, I left the instrument in my closet when I began having kids. My sons seemed determined to destroy the instrument when they were little guys. To protect it, I had to put it up. Unfortunately, it has stayed in the closet to this day. It really is hard to leave an expensive classical instrument out and about with three little energetic male children running around the house. And my kids were energetic!

Sometimes I do think about going back to guitar. Then the exigencies of life take over, and the thought disappears. "To everything there is a season and a time …" I was enriched by the guitar in its season of my life.

In high school, I began to frequent the Club 47 coffeehouse in Harvard Square in Cambridge, Massachusetts and was exposed to the ideas of the revolution that my generation anticipated would end not only Vietnam but also war itself, changing America and moving humanity toward kindness, compassion, and egalitarianism. I attended hoot-nannies with frequency in high school. In college, I frequented a commune where my ex-wife had hung out before I got to UMass in the fall of 1965. She had begun college in the summer, and I stayed in Newton to work as a bookkeeper with Auntie Rae at the cryogenics lab at MIT, where she was the administrative assistant. There my job was accounting for the shipping of liquid nitrogen around the country to labs and companies that used it. That was my summer job before college … working at MIT.

I came home from college to visit in 1965 just before I got my air force haircut. My father greeted me by putting his arm around my shoulders and saying, "Why don't you take your long hair, boots, and hippie ideas and shove them up your ass." I don't think he appreciated the cultural revolution underway. And what kind of sense did it make for me to be joining the air force but hanging out with antiwar hippies? He was confused (as was I).

My interests in ending suffering, my social concerns about capitalism and imperialism, my interests in social egalitarianism and social justice, and my understanding of unconscious determinism all seemed to be leading me into a bifurcated future in which I would be in conflict with myself, my parents, and society. Nowhere was that more clear to me than when I got to college. I was in the air force but hung out with hippies, was disciplined in classical music but played folk music, was in a behavioral psychology program but strongly adhered to psychoanalytic theory and felt that psychology's role was to create large scale social change and social justice for all rather than experimenting with rats in a lab. I was terribly conflicted and confused in my own strivings for differentiation of self. Too bad for me. Well, it was 1965, after all.

To be a sixties revolutionary or not to be? That was the question. I wanted both worlds at the same time, but I had issues with both worlds. I did not appreciate the war in Vietnam but was no pacifist. I appreciated social welfare, caring for everyone by a government, but I stopped short of accepting that the government should own the means of production. I was an oddball ... or an iconoclast. Perhaps if I had lived in California, it might have been different for the better. Half of my family lived in California (Uncle Hy and his family), and they always seemed much more laid back to me. I envied that.

As a psychology major with a premed curriculum and carrying overloaded semesters, my marks suffered. My interests were elsewhere other than my studies. Besides, I was lousy at math. This was not a good place for me to be, in a behavioral psychology department and a premed curriculum. All I wanted was to get out and pursue a career as an analyst and a social change agent. That was not to be, given my marks and the fact that I would probably not get into medical school. I knew nothing about lay analysis in college and had no guidance in those respects. But *An Elementary Textbook of Psychoanalysis* stayed on my dorm room bookshelf throughout college. It remains on my bookshelf to this very day.

I cannot blame my average marks in undergraduate school on being a misplaced student. I was too interested in my high school sweetheart, who I would marry directly after college in June 1968. In my senior year, I probably drank too much. I did not try marijuana or any other drugs. I spent too much time on the air force and not enough time on my studies. And I was too immature and confused to go to a large school like the University of Massachusetts Amherst. I still graduated in three years instead of four with a bachelor of science in psychology in 1968. I felt that accelerated program was an accomplishment despite my less than stellar GPA.

As I mentioned, I also took the premedical curriculum, as I had promised my father. I wanted out of college and to start my career. I was always in a hurry. I also did not want to go home to face the conflict, arguing, and tension in that house. When I left home for college at seventeen, I vowed to myself that I would not return to that conflict and tension in our home, and I stayed at school all year round. That is one way I graduated in three years rather than four. I received almost one semester's worth of advanced credits in German, which I attribute to my education at Newton South High School (NSHS). All of that helped me to graduate early.

In college, I did have opportunities to explore science. I fortuitously secured a research assistantship in educational psychology my freshman year (by random luck and chutzpah) studying syllogistic reasoning. In my senior year, I was fortunate to secure a technical assistantship in high-energy physics, working on an experiment to identify leptonic decay patterns (again, by random luck and chutzpah).

These opportunities meant more to me than my formal studies. Every week, the physicists for whom I was working held classes for the technical assistants on high-energy physics. I learned so much there—more than in the classroom. Physics has been a hobby and passion of mine my whole life.

Six months after graduating college and working at a Massachusetts state mental hospital, I secured (again by luck and chutzpah) a traineeship at the Lakes Region Mental Health Center (LRMHC) in Laconia, New Hampshire (NH). This was after serving in psychiatric social work at a State Mental Hospital directly after college in 1968. I began my work at the LRMHC on January 2, 1969.

In New Hampshire, at the tender age of twenty-one, I was blessed to have Anna L. Philbrook, MD, as my clinical supervisor. Anna was a great psychodynamic psychiatrist. She *was* psychiatry in New Hampshire, and the University of New Hampshire named their dining commons after her (while she was still living). She was the archetypal physician/psychiatrist, filled with intellect and compassion.

"Supervision" meant supervision/therapy. One had to investigate themselves to be able to assist others without intruding their own issues into the therapy. I learned both child and adult psychotherapy under Dr. Philbrook's instruction and guidance.

I actually carried quite a load of patients, since we had only four mental health professionals to service two counties. I got to serve on call at the ER at the regional hospital, consulted to the regional prison, and provided mental health consultation to the elementary schools in two counties. Under the supervision of our team's psychologist, I learned how to give the Wechsler Intelligence Test, the House, Tree Person projective assessment, and the Bender Gestalt Test. It was a lot for a twenty-one-year-old with only a bachelor's degree. It was a unique opportunity.

When I left New Hampshire after my term at the Lakes Region Mental Health Center in August 1970, I was well prepared for graduate school. I went to graduate school at Springfield College in Springfield, Massachusetts. I would never have gotten into graduate school without having spent the time training in New Hampshire. When I did get to graduate school, they waived my first-year courses based on my experience and an extensive recommendation of my former clinic director. I was forever grateful.

Three things happened while I was in New Hampshire that would help to get me to leave a conservative state and go to a liberal humanist graduate school in psychology: the Moratorium to End the War in Vietnam, the Woodstock Music Festival, and my public support for legalizing marijuana. I participated in the Moratorium and wore a black arm band to work. That did not sit well in the office in conservative New Hampshire. We decided to go to Woodstock, but the New York Thruway had been closed, so we never made it there. The community fathers did not appreciate my public health stance on pot and did not understand that my support of legalization was to be better able to control the substance, stop the illegal trafficking, and stop the unfair imprisonment of black and Hispanic people. I am afraid that I was seen as a radical and that my tenure in the community would be untenable. Years later, I feel that I have been vindicated by the legalization of cannabis in so many states.

I actually felt battered around by the rejection of the community for the stance I took on what I thought was a public health issue. It was serious rejection, and I was afraid that it would affect my livelihood. It was pretty frightening.

Being rejected for a political/public health policy stance was not necessarily new for me. Nor would it be the last time I would experience such a thing. But if you believe that you are correct about something, you need to stick to it.

I should not overlook the cultural anti-Semitism that I encountered at that time. It was generally subtle and sometimes overt. But it was there in my life. My Jewish paranoia was activated. I did not ever feel physically threatened, but I did feel like an outsider.

Some of that was New England stuff. You have to have been born in a place to be accepted in New England. There is a legendary story told about a person who came to Nantucket Island at age three with his family. He died at ninety-nine years old. His tombstone is said to read, "Goodbye Stranger." It's a New England thing. So I cannot chock it all up to anti-Semitism or my Jewish paranoia.

Frankly, the confluence of the idea of social change (*Wasp*), the influence of analytic psychology (*An Elementary Textbook of Psychoanalysis*), growing up in Boston and Newton, being Jewish, and experiencing the counterculture of the 1960s all contributed to what I was becoming. So, graduate school was the next horizon. New Hampshire was not going to be a long-term home for me.

It is important to note three other things that happened in the sixties that had an influence on where I was going politically and in terms of becoming a social change agent: President Kennedy was assassinated in 1963, and in 1968, both Dr. Martin Luther King Jr. and Robert Kennedy were assassinated. The social revolution was over—or never really happened. Woodstock was the beginning of the end, and the Altamont Free Concert in California was really the end. After the tragedy of Altamont, where the Hell's Angels were contracted to do security for the concert and all hell broke loose (no pun intended), the counterculture either retreated to rural areas like Vermont or Upstate NY or got jobs and joined the great capitalist middle class to become their parents.

I began to turn my attention to changing the health status of individuals and communities as the change that I thought I could professionally make. I never gave up my social values formed in the sixties. The reader will see those values play out throughout my later life in terms of supporting justice as fairness, social egalitarianism, and ethics. I chose not to retreat and not to become my parents. I followed the path of being a healer. But I did recognize that the movement was over. A socialist revolution was not going to happen. War would not end. Capitalism would continue. The poor would continue to be structurally oppressed. Institutional racism would not disappear.

I started taking master of social work (MSW) courses at Boston University during my time in New Hampshire (1969–70). At that time, BU offered graduate credit courses through the School of Social Work Institute. I discovered that I really wanted to be in graduate school in psychology and not social work. I transferred my credits to Springfield College. I loved being at Boston University though. My father had studied history there for a short time. I loved the learning, but I wanted to go to Springfield College.

Springfield was the only graduate school I really wanted to go to. I had an athletic coach at UMass who had gone to Springfield. He impressed me as a renaissance man. He was a physical education coach who could discuss philosophy and politics and psychology. I decided that any school that could produce him was where I wanted to go too. I was not disappointed.

But what do you do when you have *An Elementary Textbook of Psychoanalysis* as your guide, three years of psychodynamic training under your belt, and you attend a humanistic school? You write your master's paper on psychoanalysis, of course. At Springfield, one had the choice of a master of education (MEd) or a master of arts (MA). I selected the MEd and a synthetic paper in lieu of a thesis. I earned the MEd in counseling psychology 1971.

Because my professors were humanists and did not have much

affinity for psychodynamic theory or my paper on that subject, they sent me to a psychoanalyst to have that person grade my final work at that school. It was a very interesting oral examination. It was rather strenuous. I passed. In fact, I left Springfield with a straight A, 4.0 GPA. I was inducted into the National Honor Society of the American Psychological Society, Psi Chi. As a struggling undergraduate, I never expected that I would do so well. Charles Brenner and his little book helped me along this path.

As an undergraduate, I had done so badly in one psychology course that the professor advised me to choose any other field except psychology. I thought about that professor a lot when I passed the national board exam in psychology and received my license from the commonwealth of Massachusetts in 1978. Perhaps the past is really not prologue to the future. Perhaps there really are many possible futures. We should strive not to predict the future for students or anyone. Who knows what the end result will be? I try to remember that as a teacher.

I also owe a great debt to my major professor, Walter English, EdD (distinguished professor of humanics at Springfield College). Although a staunch humanist, Wally (as he was known to all) allowed me the space to continue to discover psychoanalysis. So, by the time I finished my master of education in counseling psychology, I had exposure to and training in psychodynamic theory, behavioral theory, and humanistic theory and practice. This was a fairly well-rounded psychological education. I was fortunate to have such a broad exposure to theory and practice.

Psychodynamics gave me insight into human behavior, but humanism helped me express my genuine human concern as a practitioner and leader. Psychodynamics helped me understand the way the mind works at the unconscious level, but humanism helped me express compassion and the reduction of suffering. With this background of both psychodynamics and humanism in hand, I landed a job as assistant director of intergroup relations for the city of Springfield, Massachusetts, in June 1971, as soon as I graduated from my master's program. It was there that I divorced my first wife and met and married my second wife, Debbie. That is a whole other story, which I will address in its time and sequence.

I do not want the reader to conclude that I became an entirely psychodynamic-oriented psychologist. I did not. My training in humanism at Springfield College had a profound effect on me. While I credit the US Air Force with teaching me the bureaucratic side of administration, it was my humanistic background that made me ready for humanistic management. I bought the idea that the "proper study of mankind is man."[14] I bought the idea that democracy was a great system for ensuring the rights of every person, even within the workplace. But I also bought the concepts of social welfare and socialism (socialism light) to ensure that everyone is taken care of to the highest degree possible within a society. This is true within organizations as well as in society as a whole.

I was chief executive officer at the Greater New Bedford Community Health Center, Inc. (GNBCHC) from 1990 to 2007. I went to many funerals of my staff and their families. I wanted my staff to know that I cared about them. My door was always open, and everyone from the CFO to the janitor came in. I treated no one differently, and my staff knew it. I did management by walking around and sat and talked with my employees about their lives and their concerns. I cared about my staff. In other words, I was a humanistic manager, and I carried that forward in every organization I ever ran, from Center for Alcohol and Substance Abuse Disorders (CASAD; 1977–88),to the Prevention and Access to Care and Treatment (PACT) Project at Brigham and Women's Hospital(2009),to the Jewish Community Alliance of Northeastern Pennsylvania (2016–17). I was a humanistic administrator because of who I am and because I am a graduate of Springfield College.

In my original list of books, *Getting to Yes* by Fisher, Ury, and Patton had a place on the bookshelf. Even though it did not make it into the fourteen books, it is a book illustrative of my humanistic concerns. Getting to the win-win in conflict management has been my hallmark as an administrator. This is humanism at work. After I took the course on principled negotiation at the BU School of Social Work, I bought a bunch of *Getting to Yes* books and brought them back to my organization for all of my managers to read. Well, that did not work well, but it was a good try. I still believe in the win-win.

In conclusion, understanding the concept of unconscious determinism had a profound effect on me. Since reading Charles Brenner's book, I always sought out the causes of people's behaviors ... mine included. Sometimes this irritated my friends and family. Introspection is good, but you do not have to express its conclusions all over the place. I am still learning the art of keeping one's mouth under control. As the saying goes, "Everything that is thought, need not be said. Everything that is said, need not be written, everything that is written, need not be published." As my good friend and mentor Charles (Charlie) Barnes, PhD, told me, "You should always tell the truth, but you do not have to tell it all over the place."

Understanding unconscious determinism is both a blessing and curse. It is good to know what motivates people, but it is not always helpful to communicate those facts. Nor does such knowledge always change one's behavior. Sometimes it works, and sometimes it doesn't. Still, I would rather have the insights than not.

Analytic reasoning and awareness have shaped my perceptions of people and life since I first read Charles Brenner's book.

Behavior rests on factors we are not always aware of.

The Wisdom of Laotse by Lin Yutang, 1966

Therefore, hardness and stiffness are the companions of death,
  And softness and gentleness are the companions of life.[15]

The *Tao Te Ching* is the central writing of Chinese Taoism. It was
written, purportedly, by Lao Tzu in the sixth century BCE in Hunan
Province in China. As a version of the story goes, Lao Tzu was the chief
librarian in Hunan, and his wisdom was known far and wide. When
the emperor heard of Lao Tzu, he dispatched Confucius to find him.
Confucius met Lao Tzu and reported back to the emperor by saying,
"I have met Lao Tzu, and he is the Dragon." At this, the emperor
legendarily sent troops to kill Lao Tzu.

   Lao Tzu heard of this and began to leave the city at night. Stopped
by the gatekeeper, he was not let to pass the gate of the city until he wrote
down his wisdom. Lao Tzu sat down and wrote the eighty-one chapters
of the *Tao Te Ching* and gave it to the gatekeeper. He then road off on
his water buffalo never to be seen again. Many pictures of Lao Tzu depict
him riding on a water buffalo.

   How much of this legend is true or not, no one knows. It is a great
story, however. I relate it as it was related to me and not as it may appear
in other scholarly texts.

   I knew of Lao Tzu in college. My first and only cat was named Lao after Lao Tzu. My ex-wife and I got him as a kitten in Concord, New Hampshire, in 1969, and I had Lao for eleven years. He was a beautiful chocolate Siamese cat. He used to stand guard over my first son in his crib and later in front of the door to his room, protecting him from who knows what. He was one loyal cat!

Lao Tzu had disciples, and his main disciple, Chuang Tzu, wrote further explanations of the wisdom of the Tao. Taoism merged with Buddhism sometime in the twelfth century CE to become Zen and was imported to Japan. Tao and Zen Buddhism are fundamental philosophies to the Oriental martial arts. The *Tao Te Ching* became like a religious book to me, and I carried a copy of it everywhere.

From 1975 to 1985, I was a very serious student of the martial arts and Oriental philosophies. I revisited the Tao that I had first discovered in college, during my studies of the martial arts. I studied Kenpo, Japanese Jujitsu, Jeet Kune Do, kickboxing, and much later Tai Chi. I achieved a brown belt in Kenpo and Jujitsu(1977) and a black belt in kickboxing (Kune Do format) in 1979. I loved the ideas of quietism that Taoism preached. I needed to cultivate such quietism, given the nature of my crazy life and the anxiety I carried around with me. Meditation, a central part of Zenism, helped somewhat as well. I yearned for a life of contemplative mental quietude, but I never achieved it.

There is a difference between wanting and doing. Quietism is a great goal, especially if you do not have children, a job, financial responsibilities, and so on. If you are a monk, well that is more suited to that kind of quest. But that does not mean that one cannot appreciate the quest and participate in it. One must be realistic, however. One can strive toward quietism. With a family and a profession, however, it is more difficult to achieve.

The Tao's philosophy is brilliant. For me, it has always been more of a *striving toward* than an acquisition of quietism. Tao is one of the underlying concepts behind the Oriental martial arts. The arts, to me, are not about fighting but are rather vehicles for self-understanding and personal development.

The principles of Tao that most affected me include the following:

- life is a series of interacting, complementary polarities as expressed by yin/yang
- *tzu-jan* (by itself, so), the concept that things happen on their own
- *wu-we*, noninterference in the course of things or letting things be
- *te*, or the harmony of all things existing together in balance
- *li*, or the primacy of experiencing the world
- the metaphor of being like water in that softness belies its strength

I find these concepts all virtuous to strive toward and very hard to attain.

When Bruce Lee wrote the *Tao of Jeet Kune Do* (a book formative to me as a martial artist and on my list of the original thirty-seven books), he incorporated the concepts of Taoism and Zenism. Combining Buddhism and Tao was a feat accomplished in China long after the Buddhist monk Bodhidharma brought Buddhism to China from India. Both philosophical disciplines had some similar goals—noninterference or detachment and the reduction of or end of suffering through nonattachment.

These principles are overwhelmingly important to all people, East and West. As such, although this might sound counterintuitive, the fighting arts are really about the reduction of suffering and the increase of compassion. The martial arts are not about fighting. The martial arts are vehicles to self-understanding … in the ideal.

There are a plethora of books on these subjects. Alan Watt's book *What Is Tao* certainly should be in any serious Oriental philosophy student's library. So too books by Shuniyo Suzuki as well as Okakura's *The Book of Tea*, and the list goes on and on in this area of rich literature and wisdom.

If it had not been for the arts and these philosophies of being, I would have had a much harder time getting through my father's death. I also would have had a much harder time getting through the entire 1980s! Taoism and Zenism can lead to a sense of peace with the world and with oneself. So, it is not surprising that many people of my generation gravitated toward these philosophies. These were helpful concepts to me, but because of the depth of my personal conflicts, these were still not enough of a salve.

The Tao also taught me that letting things be is important, versus actual accomplishment. Quietism is not something you just learn and do. One must practice and cultivate it. Integrating it into your life as a Westerner is no easy task either. Its lessons are eternal and critical but extremely difficult to do. It is easier if you are not attached to anything (ala Buddhism). That is a high bar for Americans living in a competitive capitalist society. Taoism is a path worthy of our attention. It certainly has held my attention for years.

I strive to be better at the Tao, and that is the very problem I face in the process. Tao is more about being than about striving. That creates a paradox for Western people. In Tao, it is being that is important. When you strive toward something, you destroy the process of being. As the Zen saying goes, "When you seek it, you cannot find it."

My format of approach to life as a young person was emotional (if not at times classically hysterical). I had a good chunk of anxiety, as I have mentioned. I often anticipated the outcome before even beginning a project. I internalized my father's rejection and anticipated rejection in life. That is not a good format for success. I knew that this was a struggle that I would have to address throughout my life. When I found Tao, I thought that it could be a helpful part of the solution.

Training yourself to be quiet and to let things take their course is not easy. It requires mentorship, guidance, and practice. I do not want the reader to feel that I am a master of letting things take their course. Although I tried to study the Tao, I did not have a lot of success at being a good Taoist. This is something I have to work on every day ... sometimes better than others and sometimes worse. And you need mentors. I was so very lucky to have two colleagues at work at Rutland Heights Hospital who became my good friends and who served as mentors in the arts and in Oriental philosophy for me. One, my supervisor, was a new Kenpo student, and my other colleague had a black belt in Kenpo. Of course, I chose to study Kenpo.

My learning about Tao and Zen was very much helped along and directed by my friends. A number of years later, one of these men became my martial arts instructor, and I earned my black belt under his guidance. It was great to have such people in my life who could help guide me in the oriental arts and philosophy. I feel very fortunate to have had these two friends in my life. I have learned so much from both of them. One who was my martial arts instructor is now deceased, and the other remains my close friend to this day.

As happened in China, when Buddhism and Taoism merged to become Zen Buddhism, such was the case for me as well. My studies merged both Buddhism and Zen. But this is a process. It does not and did not happen for me overnight or even over a few years. Practicing shedding attachments to the world to relieve suffering and being quiet in response to the rush of life is not easy. You cannot do it alone, even if the changes required are internal. You cannot be a rogue martial artist. I am not sure that you can be a rogue anything. People need a community.

The title of this text reflects the issues of following Tao and how difficult that is to accomplish. When you try to follow Tao, you learn quickly that this is a process and that one can strive toward it. But you have to be unattached from the goal to achieve it. "When you seek it, you cannot find it." While I am attached to striving, it is the effort of striving itself that may be the blockage. This is where East and West may not see things quite the same.

There is the story of one who wanted to become a black belt. He found the greatest instructor and asked how long the process would take. "Ten years," replied the master.

"Master," said the student, "that is a long time. What if I come to dojo (kwon) every day?"

"Twenty years," said the master.

"Master," said the student, "twenty years is a very long time. What if I fight every student in the dojo (kwon) every day?"

"Thirty years," said the master.

"Master," inquired the student, "how come every time that I tell you I will work harder, you tell me it will take longer?"

The master answered, "When one eye is fixed on the goal, there is only one eye left to see the way."

Another story I value is about self-definition. This is something I have already noted as an important psychological issue. One day a student went to the abbot of his monastery and complained, "Master, I do not know who I am."

"Do you see the door?" said the master.

"Yes, Master," said the student, "I see the door."

"You are the one who is looking at the door," said the master.

As the song in the film *Frozen* says, "Let it go."

"Striving is everything" (in Western culture). And yet life is the journey of working toward a goal without being attached to that process or its actual accomplishment. This has been a great lesson for me in my life. While it is good in the West to have goals, those goals themselves may be deterrents. In Taoism, striving can be a goal and a blockage. Just the act of striving itself can be an anti-Taoist approach.

My life has been a dynamic tension between Greek Western thought, Judaic thought, and Taoist/Buddhist thought. Sometimes a person embraces one, and sometimes another. This is the yin and yang of my life. Recognizing that there are complementary polarities in life does not necessarily resolve the dichotomies between them. Letting things be as they are takes great effort, when it is actually no effort that is required. Is this not similar to psychoanalysis in that knowing about unconscious motivations is important but might not actually change anything just through its knowing?

How does one strive while letting go of striving and outcomes? This is one of the great dilemmas of my life ... and a curious paradoxical absurdity.

JB by Archibald MacLeish, 1965

> If god is god he is not good. If god is good he is not god.
> Take the even, take the odd. I would not sleep here if I
> could except for the little green leaves in the wood and
> the wind on the water.[16]

I am not quite sure how, when, or why I became engaged with the problem of absurdity and theodicy, but I did. Perhaps it was my concern about the Holocaust. Perhaps it was my family life. Perhaps it was the result of conflicted parental relationships.

In college, I was introduced to *JB* by Archibald MacLeish in my freshman year in English class (I believe). I did see the play performed at UMass. *JB* is a play expounding the modern retelling of the biblical book of Job. As such, it contains themes of theodicy and of absurdity. And it is absurdity that is a concern of existentialism. My interest in existentialism can be seen by reviewing my original thirty-seven-book list, which contains works of Sartre and Camus. But, on reflection, it is *JB* that first made my fourteen-book list, representing the concept of theodicy.

Theodicy is the question of how a just and merciful god can allow evil to exist. Great lines that I appreciate from this play *JB* follow:

> If god is good he is not god. If god is god he is not good.
> Take the even, take the odd. I would not sleep here if I

could, except for the little green leaves in the wood and
the wind on the water.[17]

I read those words in *JB* as a freshman and flipped out. I memorized
the lines, and I still say them today when discussing theodicy.

For me, theodicy is the single most important question of theo-
philosophy to be answered today. The entire history of the Jewish people
revolves around this question. After the Holocaust (Shoah), this is the
great question we are left with. It is a great question of existentialism as
well. It is the question that has plagued me my entire life. How can god
be merciful and compassionate with so much evil in the world? How
indeed? And how can people select to worship such a god?

I actually was not just concerned with human tragedy and suffering.
The entire animal world is filled with suffering. What kind of deity
would create such a world where everything eats everything else, where
nature is "red in tooth and claw,"[18] and where there is unimaginable
cruelty and suffering? It cannot be very pleasant to be a zebra being eaten
alive by lions on the savannah of Africa. What kind of creationism grand
design is this? It made me angry at such a deity.

I know that there are those who will say that God's ways are not our
ways and we cannot understand the design that only God understands. I
think that is a cop-out. Suffering is suffering, and it is not a good thing.
If this is the kind of God that we worship for his allowance of cruelty,
then both God and we need a psychiatrist—God for His behavior,
and human beings for their worship of such a deity. Okay, I know that
makes me a heretic. But I do consider that what we mean by the word
god requires full definition. God is a concept that we define for ourselves.
How we define the word dictates how we relate to it.

The biblical book of Job is great literature in and of itself. It is
an ancient text trying to unravel what has lasted through millennia
to become a modern question. To read the same theodicy issues in a
modern play like *JB* had a great effect on me. This was not a religious
text or the Bible. It was modern literature by a modern playwright. And

I was not coming to this in religious training but in college and in a secular setting.

JB profoundly affected me and crystallized my sense of the absurd. But if the theodicy question was absurd, what of religion itself? This deeply troubled me. I was a fairly religious fellow, trying to find his religious and intellectual way. I had a deep sense of commitment to and appreciation of the Jewish people and the Jewish religion, based in my relationship with my maternal grandfather (Harry J. Levin) as my mentor, as well as the entire community in which I grew up.

"HiPop," as I called him,[19] took me to services at a shtetl-type shul across the street from our apartment at 35 Michigan Avenue in Boston when I was five or six years old. My grandmother (Nana, as I called her, or Ida Ostroff Levin) had bought me a little tallit to wear to shul. My grandparents were so proud to show me off. I remember that day as if it were yesterday. The old men (probably all in their forties) with beards, smelling of tobacco, sat around the perimeter of the little shul. The women sat behind a black curtain, where they could be heard but not seen. The bimah was in the center, and the aron kodesh with rampant lions of Judah flanking each side of the Ten Commandments tablet on the wall over the ark in the tradition of an Orthodox shul. This was my first shul experience, and I loved it. I loved being with my grandfather. I loved my new tallit. I loved the admiration of the "old" men. I felt accepted and at home. I felt a sense of belonging and safety.

But at home, when I asked my mother what god was, I got a surprising answer. You see, my mother was a pantheist, and to her, everything was god. This was disturbing to me as a child. It is a position I grew to appreciate as an adult. I wanted a more definitive answer. And although my grandfather went to shul, he was a card-carrying Zionist/socialist. That meant that he was also most likely an atheist. He was a cultural Jew but never spoke about god at all. We observed the holidays and made brachot (blessings), but we never really spoke about God. Neither did my father or his parents. Auntie Rae was an admitted agnostic at least and atheist at most. Still, she studied Hebrew and went on aliyah to Israel.

I did not recognize any of this as socialist Zionism when I was a kid or how it would affect me later on in life.

So, where did that leave me? I got the Zionism part. I even got the socialism and community parts. I just misinterpreted the cultural aspects of tradition and holidays as a deep belief in God. It was really a deep appreciation for the Jewish people, the nation of Israel. I was not old enough to recognize that the JNF (Jewish National Fund) blue and white charity box and the *Forward* (newspaper) in Yiddish were not signs of devout religion but of Jewish national and cultural self-determination.

My paternal grandparents were Eastern European Jews, as were my maternal grandparents. Harry (Grandpa) Forman and Fanny (Bubbie) Forman did not really keep kosher like my maternal grandparents. They were Rush (Russians). My step-grandmother (Bubbie) was descended from rabbis and spoke five languages besides Yinglish (Russian, Yiddish, Polish, German, and Hebrew). My grandfather was a much simpler man who worked in a shoe factory. They came to this country to escape prejudice, persecution, and pogroms and to find a better economic life. I am not sure that they came especially to practice radical monotheistic Judaism but rather to be able to be *living* Jews instead of *dead* Jews.

In Hebrew school, at a Conservative shul, I tended toward those of greater observance. My parents did not have a mezuzah on the door, did not keep kosher or keep Shabbat, and only attended services twice a year on Rosh Hashanah and Yom Kippur. They lit candles on Hanukkah and had a Passover Seder. They did not ever celebrate Sukkoth or Shavuot or Simchat Torah or Tisha B'Av. I put the mezuzah up on my parents' house and insisted on lighting Shabbat candles. "Where did he come from?" was my parents' lament about my Jewishness.

That was as far as my parents would let me go. Saturdays were golf days for my father. When he came home, we made Italian sandwiches for lunch with ham, mortadella, salami, cheese, pimento, olives, and oil. Yum. Treyf (not kosher) but yummy.

So there I was, an orthopraxis Jew in a Zionist/socialist/ (maybe) atheist household and not knowing it. Along with religiosity came theological questioning as well. I was religious because I thought that was what my grandfather was all about and because my teachers and Jewish mentors were observant. But that was apparently a misinterpretation of my own family.

My family were proud Jews, but they were assimilating American Jews. They could not understand my interest in theology or in religiosity. And I felt strongly about those things. They did not. I believe that it troubled them. After all, they had grown up in an era where there was a simple equation ... Jew equals dead. Both of my grandmothers survived pogroms in Russia and in Lithuania. I only assume that was true for my grandfathers also, although they never talked about it.

Of course, I joined Hillel (the Jewish student organization) in college. Of course, I participated in the Tallit and Tephillin club in my dorm. Of course, I attended services at college. And, of course, *JB* became a formative book for me. That was because underneath my religious observance was a family of Zionist/socialist/atheists/agnostics in hiding. *JB* represented the conflicts of the theodicy question and of absurdity. What could be more absurd than Eastern European Jews in America? The quote from *JB* above resonated with me, although I would not find answers acceptable to me until much later in life.

The absurdity of my college life reflected my inner conflicts and paradoxes. UMass had about five hundred Jews in the student body of about twelve thousand at the Amherst Campus. It was not very comfortable. I joined the air force and took ROTC. Nice young Jewish boys ("NJBs") did not do that in 1965. Nice Jewish boys in 1965 were striving to become doctors or lawyers or businessmen. My air force friends were predominantly Christian. Only a few of my friends were Jewish, and we did band together. It was not like campus was anti-Semitic, but it was not exactly comfortable either. It was only slightly absurd within my conscious awareness. Discomfort can breed a recognition of the absurd, however. And because birds of a feather flock together, the Jewish kids stayed together as much as possible.

So, *JB* was the appetizer to my study of absurdity, existentialism, and the meaning of life. It was also the segue into a lifelong quest to unravel the theodicy question and to come to grips with my own Judaism. I wish that I had come to grips with all of that before I had a family! It would have been easier on my sons.

As I write this, I am in a conversation with a cousin as to the possibility of God being both a noun and a verb at the same time. People just do not like the idea of God being either impotent or evil in accordance with the theodicy question. They also do not like the idea of praying to a verb. Yet if God is a verb and not a noun, then the theodicy question need not trouble us so much.

In this quest, I have been influenced by Kabbalistic theory. My major professor in my master of science in Jewish studies program was the venerable Rabbi Byron L. Sherwin, PhD, a great Kabbalistic scholar. I was also influenced by the work of people such as Rabbi David Cooper and Jay Michaelson. I would add to this the current work of Carlo Rovelli, the theoretical physicist.

I appreciate the idea that understanding being is to understand things as a set of events rather than of discrete things. I appreciate the concept that there maybe no universal reality but rather just local realities defined in relationship to one another in a bubble of time, space, and reality.

I appreciate language as being inadequate to define either reality or god. Yet language is a tool we have to express awe. I also appreciate that our language about the term *god* reflects the concepts that God is our definition of everything and that everything can only be defined in relationship to everything else. *God* is the process of the universe and not the idea of the universe as a *thing* itself.

Relevant to the biblical book of Job and the play *JB*, theodicy has no answer. If God is a noun and cannot intervene in evil, then God must not be omnipotent. If God as a noun can intervene in evil but selects not to, then God is evil. If, however, god is defined as a verb, this kind of takes God off the hook for evil. It is hard to get angry at a process.

My takeaway is that *there is no answer to theodicy as long as our conception of God is that God is a noun.* I prefer the verb idea.

Catch-22 by Joseph Heller, 1966

And what difference does that make?[20]

If religion was a conflicted area for me, so were war, cruelty, and human beings' unending capacity to harm one another.

I went to college during the Vietnam War. I incongruously and rather inexplicably wanted to join the US Air Force Reserve and take the Reserve Officers' Training Corps program to become a commissioned officer. My parents, especially my father, did not want to sign the papers for me to go into military service (I was seventeen years old and needed parental permission for the military). When I went to him with the authorization papers, he told me that war was futile. Where was he my whole life? I questioned. My entire childhood had been filled with stories of WWII and how the army had been the best years for my parents. Sure they were. They never left Alabama and Ft. McClellan. My father was retained at the fort as a medic in the induction station when his unit shipped out to be killed to a man at invasion of Anzio, Italy. He had survivor guilt and kept a picture of his company over his desk his entire life.

But the war was actually the best time for my parents. As I understand, they lived in off-post housing, drank and entertained a lot, lived for the moment, and my father played golf on post. What was so bad? Around them, WWII and the Holocaust raged, and across the pond, my uncles were fighting. They met in the Battle of the Bulge.

As opposed to my father's military experience, my uncle's service time was not so good. My uncle Morry was in the infantry division pinned down in the Battle of the Bulge. My uncle Hy was in a tank recon unit in General Patton's Third Armored Division, which was called upon to relieve the infantry from the grips of Hitler's armies. When my uncle Morry heard which units were coming to assist them, he got permission to sit in a tree and watch the tanks roll in to see if he could find his brother, Hy. It was winter. As the story goes, Hy was sitting on top of a tank, and Uncle Morry spotted him. They met in combat. Hy sent letters back home describing the meeting, and it was written up in *Army Times* newspaper as to how two brothers met in combat.

As Uncle Hy's unit was moving out, his tank was blown up. He lost his hearing and had a permanent limp thereafter. He was evacuated from the field to England and then back to the US. His war was over, but his brother proceeded on through Germany. In a history book my father had, Uncle Morry had written an inscription, "I won WWII!" He brought home *souvenirs* that suggested that his war was up close and personal.

Knowing my uncles, I had a hard time envisioning them as soldiers. I certainly had a hard time envisioning them killing people. Both were very mild men. I especially had a hard time envisioning Morry in combat. But his war booty belied that impression. He brought home a Nazi dirk emblazoned with a swastika, a Nazi flag, and a Walther PPK taken off a dead soldier. Neither of my uncles ever spoke of the war.

But, for my parents, life was good in Alabama in WWII. It all seemed so ludicrous and absurd.

Despite knowing all of these stories, I still wanted to join the service. I wanted my father's respect as a soldier as he and his brothers had been. They had their war (WWII), and Vietnam was my generation's war. I certainly did not want the ordeal of war, but I did want the respect as a soldier and an officer. I also thought I wanted to fly airplanes. Young idealistic men do not think through being in combat very well. "Dulce et decorum est, pro patria more." Isn't that a way to gain your father's respect if he had been a soldier?

My parents finally did sign for me to join the air force after much consternation. Vietnam was raging. It was 1965.

Then I read *Catch-22* in my freshman year. If anything captured the futility and absurdity of war, it was *Catch-22*. I heard Joseph Heller read the book, and I saw the movie with Alan Arkin and Art Garfunkel. It was an expression of the absurdity about war as a metaphor for life. And life is absurd.

Absurdity was my experience of life. It was absurd that my father was so angry and verbally abusive toward those he loved the most. It was absurd that I was so religious within a family of atheist/agnostics. It was absurd that I was in the air force but hung out with the hippies who were against the war in Vietnam. It was absurd that I could not answer the theodicy question. It was absurd that I was taking coursework I had little affinity for. It was absurd that I wanted to be a psychoanalyst but was in a behavioral school. It was absurd that I was going to marry a woman I continually argued with and would divorce. And on the dichotomies went.

(As I was writing this, the Public Broadcasting System's "Great Book Read" was going on to establish the most beloved novel in America. One hundred books had already been selected. *Catch-22* was one of them.)

Yet, despite all of this, I was in the Air Force Reserve. Because I had accelerated my academic program, however, I could not attend survival field training when it was scheduled between my junior and senior years. I was out of sequence with the ROTC schedule and could not take my air force commission unless I was on schedule with the air force program. That would require me to complete college in four years, including survival training as scheduled. I had to be in school during the summer during the time the air force had scheduled me to take that training module.

I tried to transfer into the army after college. I was supposed to go to officer candidate school (OCS) but popped an inguinal hernia, which prevented my attendance. Later in 1969, I received a medical deferment for a heart condition (Wolff-Parkinson-White syndrome).

Being commissioned and on active duty was just not going to happen for me, despite my desire and efforts toward that goal.

I did receive an honorable discharge from the United States Air Force Reserve, and I am proud of that fact. I was proudly air force, even if not on active-duty assignment. It was still no fun being in uniform on campus during Vietnam. As a cadet captain and wing information officer, my job was to keep the air force positive in the public eye. This was not an easy task during Vietnam.

Much later in life, I became a civilian consultant in the Social Actions Program to the Eighth Air Force, Ninety-Ninth Bomb Wing at Westover AFB on behalf of the city of Springfield when I was assistant director of intergroup relations there. When I was at Rutland Height Hospital, I specialized in combat trauma and PTSD as a psychologist and created the only public health program (not VA) for combat Vietnam veterans. Although I never saw service in Vietnam, I did devote myself to helping combat Veterans. While I was against the war, I was not necessarily against the warriors. I was never a pacifist, but I was no hawk either. And to answer your question, yes, I did treat those who created atrocities as well as those who survived them.

By 1968, I had become against the War in Vietnam and later participated in the 1969 Moratorium to End the War. No matter how you cut it, "war is a public health catastrophe" (to quote myself in the first line of my article on PTSD referenced below).

About this time, my college roommate went to Vietnam. I experienced the war through his letters home from combat. These were frank and explicit letters that helped me to identify with what he was experiencing as a soldier. We have remained close our entire lives. This is one of the long-term relationships I refer to in this text. It has lasted fifty-five years thus far.

That war is absurd is captured in *Catch-22*. *Catch-22* became a seminal book for me. Its antiwar and existentialist themes captured my attention. It was another segue into existentialism and to becoming antiwar later on. It represented the absurdity of war and the absurdity of my own life. I identified with it. It was later that I read Sartre and Camus

(I did read *The Plague* in high school) and learned about the theatre of the absurd and saw plays by Beckett. I became an existentialist in college. How consistent with my generation but probably inconsistent with my military participation!

Life is absurd, *but one must carry on*. That was my life. How British! How Boston anglophile! It was not comfortable, but that is how my life seemed, and *Catch-22* was my open door to examining all of those issues. After all, *Catch-22* is not just about war; it is about life as a whole. It is about carrying on in the face of the absurd. It is about living with paradoxes. It is about finding one's path in the midst of the ridiculous.

Catch-22 also tries to answer the age-old question, "Why me?" The author's answer is essentially, "Why anybody?" The paradox Yossarian, the protagonist in *Catch-22*, must resolve is that while the war is indeed happening to everyone, it is happening to him. He knows that others are affected by the war, yet that does not help him. It is he who is suffering existential anxiety, and it is he who has his own catch-22 to resolve. That resonated with my own experiences in life.

His paradox is clearly portrayed in the movie by taking some artistic license with the book. Yossarian does not want to fly anymore. But the only way that he can get off of flight status is to be crazy. If he asks to be taken of flight status because they (the enemy) are shooting at him, then that request would be rationale. If he is not crazy, as evidenced by his normal fear, then he is not crazy and cannot be taken off flight status. Catch-22. I think we all feel this at one time or another when faced with our own adversities."War is hell,"[21] and so is life.

I identified with Yossarian. I had a sense of being caught up in the senseless. I did not understand my own life yet. But what I did understand was that I wanted to relieve my own pain and suffering and assist others in doing so. As Hillel tells us in *Pirke Avot*, "If I am not for myself, who will be for me? And if I am for myself only, what am I? And if not now, when?" Those words of Jewish ethics have been with me my entire life.

As I have said, my aversion to war and its suffering never made me into a pacifist. By the end of 1968, I was against the war in Vietnam, but I was not antimilitary. One can be against a war but not the warrior. Warriors can be as much victims of war as anyone else. Still, I do believe in such things as just wars. This might seem paradoxical, but it is quite consistent with my belief system.

So, what did I learn from *Catch-22*? I think I learned to value more the Buddhist parable of the house of the burning roof in the Lotus Scripture. In that parable, the Buddha relates how he tried to save people in a house with a roof that was burning. As they ruminated on what it would be like to leave their house, the Buddha left. There was nothing left to say or do.

Today, as a seventy-two-year-old with metastatic cancer, I find myself just walking away from situations that cause me more aggravation than I wish to contend with. Cancer cells do not like aggravation, and sometimes the better part of valor is to just walk away.

War can be a metaphor for life. We are all at war with something. Life is absurd, but one must carry on …

The Sirens of Titan by Kurt Vonnegut, 1966

I was a victim of a series of accidents, as are we all.[22]

I read most of Kurt Vonnegut's work during college. Like Joseph Heller, he was another WWII GI whose experiences seem to have informed his writings. War affected Vonnegut's perspectives. Vonnegut was captured in the Battle of the Bulge[23] and was a prisoner of war (POW) in Dresden during the bombing. Perhaps that is why he created the "chrono-synclastic infundibula" in both *The Sirens of Titan* and *Slaughterhouse Five*. If any sane person experienced the Battle of the Bulge, was a German POW, and witnessed and survived the bombing of Dresden, that person would probably have wished to escape earth in something like Vonnegut's chrono-synclastic infundibula too. War and suffering can make people want to escape living in the reality of the present.

Although my father used to tell me that "there are no atheists in a foxhole," I do know other vets who completely lost faith, developing the idea that whatever God would allow the evils of war was probably indifferent at least, or did not exist at most. Vonnegut created the "Church of God the Utterly Indifferent" in his book *The Sirens of Titan*. The absurdity of war that Heller describes so well is combined with the theodicy question in Vonnegut's *Sirens of Titan*.

I have already related how important theodicy had become for me at an early age. Existentialism, too, had become important, as one can see by my selection of *JB*, *Catch-22*, and *The Sirens of Titan*. These books' ideas resonated with my own sense of absurdity and concerns about theodicy. Vonnegut masterfully interwove these philosophical issues into the idea of randomness that would catch my full fancy later in life. And although I still wanted to maintain the concept of God as that ultimate reality that might intervene in the world to save people, I knew in my heart that this was not the case. How and why would God change the laws of physics on behalf of certain selected people?

"I was a victim of a series of accidents, as are we all" are Vonnegut's watchwords of the Church of God the Utterly Indifferent. He sees the idea of a caring god as an illusion. It might be a salving illusion but is an illusion nonetheless. That is why he put into the mouth of his character the Reverend C. Horner Redwine, the rector of the Church of God the Utterly Indifferent, the following words relevant to God's apathy toward human beings and the world he purportedly created: "No longer can a fool … point to a ridiculous accident of luck and say 'Somebody up there likes me.'"[24] And Reverend Redwine further admonishes Vonnegut's protagonist not to say the words "Thank God," lest he cause a riot among the believers of the Church of God the Utterly Indifferent!

As an eighteen-year-old college student, I loved Kurt Vonnegut's works. I love them still today. Vonnegut has a sense of the absurd but also a sense of randomness. Things happen. Our degree of agency and free will are probably less than we would like to think. The universe works on its own, and we are the recipients of those universal actions, whether we feel that we can influence them or not. The great Tao unfolds itself as it will. That is one of Taoism's great understandings about the universe. Contention is often not helpful. It might be that we have the illusion of free will only and that our real ability to influence things is far more limited than we would like to believe.

The watchword of Israel, "Hear O Israel, the Lord our God, the Lord is One," juxtaposes to the watchword of the Church of God the Utterly Indifferent ("I was a victim of a series of accidents, as are we all") in an interesting way. They are not necessarily inconsistent to the degree that acknowledging the oneness of God does not necessarily rule out that the universe operates according to principles of randomness and probability. Both biblical and Rabbinic Judaism propose a creator deity that, in fact, cares about the affairs of humans. This was not the god of Spinoza or Einstein, however. It is not my god either.

I think it is entirely possible to believe in a unity principle to the universe in which everything is connected to everything else. It is also quite possible to simultaneously believe in the universe being governed through the mathematics of probabilities and randomness. If there is a god at all, then I can only accept that there is one of it. If God is everything, then that still does not obviate the laws of physics. And the laws of at least one pillar of physics is quantum mechanics, which is governed by random order and probabilities. But if you say that God directs the universe through cause and effect, then I should have to ask, "As evidenced by what?" I amnot sure that either Heller or Vonnegut saw the great invisible hand at work in the background of human endeavor.

There is a certain cognitive dissonance between my appreciation of existentialism and my attachment to a more orthopraxis Judaism. These two competing forces would have to be rectified sometime during my lifetime for the sake of my mental peace. But even in my darkest hours, when I prayed fervently to God for salvation from my ills, I still quoted Vonnegut: "I was a victim of a series of accidents, as are we all." I was a paradox filled with cognitive dissonance. I may still be experienced by others as a paradox or as an iconoclast. I am not quite sure which. I think I might be a paradox to myself.

An example might be in the Joshua story in the Bible. In my rational mind, I considered the case of God stopping the sun from moving to allow Joshua to fight longer at the Battle of Jericho in the Hebrew scripture. First of all, this idea is geocentric and not heliocentric. To actually stop the sun from moving, it would be the earth that would have to stop rotating. Were that to happen, everything would fly off the earth at terminal velocity speed. And this would have serious consequences for the moon and even for other planets in our solar system. In other words, it is not only illogical, but it is so highly improbable that such a series of events would happen. It is absurd to think that such occurred just so Joshua could destroy the city (of Jericho) of indigenous people living in the land that the Israelites were ordered by God to conquer so that they could invade and claim that land for their own.

So many other instances exist to cause skepticism about divine intervention in changing the laws of physics to benefit certain people. When considered as a whole, the notion is illogical, improbable, and irrational. The default position, that God knows better than we do, is an inadequate response. Yet billions of faithful persons believe this. Accepting myths as if they were facts has been a serious problem for me to try to resolve throughout my lifetime as a person, as an educator, and as a theologian.

Even if billions of people have a belief, that does not mean that the belief is true or that you have to personally believe it.

I remember an incident in metal-working class in junior high when we were asked to draw on paper how we would fold a sheet of metal to make a box. All of the other students drew the box as a three-dimensional cube. I drew the pattern for folding the flat sheet of metal as a two-dimensional figure. My friends made fun of me. When I went home and asked my parents about my drawing, they did not say right or wrong. They said, "Do what you think is correct."

As it turned out, my pattern was the correct answer to this homework assignment. I was right, and all of my student classmates were wrong. I got an A on the assignment.

This was a huge lesson about life as well as about metal working. It was also an approach I appreciated that my parents took to teach me the lesson of standing up for what you believe. This would translate into ethical decisions later in life. I actually have the history of leaving certain jobs rather than doing something that I would consider as immoral. Much of that dates back to my story about metal work in junior high.

When I graduated from the University of Massachusetts with my degree in psychology, I got a job at a state mental hospital in psychiatric social work. At that time, the Commonwealth of Massachusetts had determined to deinstitutionalize the mental health system. That meant

that hundreds of patients at the state hospital I worked at would be placed
out into the community. My job was to help effect those placements.

Of course, as a twenty-year-old new graduate in 1968, working
in a state mental hospital was quite shocking. The conditions there
were not what one might call ideal for recovery from mental illness.
Placement into the community was a very hard job. The outpatient
system was not fully capable of receiving so many people with such
profound disturbances. There were not enough nursing homes or
halfway house beds to accommodate the numbers of people to be let
out of state hospitals. It was quite rigorous work.

Working conditions were tough on staff as well as patients. The
armamentarium of drugs for mental illnesses was somewhat limited.
The number of staff was limited. The wards seemed crowded. Everyone
did the best they could, but resources were strained, staff was tired if not
overwhelmed, and many patients were not ready to leave the hospital.

One patient who deeply impressed me was an Italian fellow who had
been in the hospital since Prohibition (it was 1968 when I worked there).
His condition was listed as "catatonic schizophrenia." His chart was one
long list of "no change" notes. He stared out a window with bars on it.
He never talked. He was now elderly.

I noticed that he had a yellowed Italian newspaper in his back pocket
that he occasionally would take out and read. So, one day, I said to him,
"Comesta?"

He smiled at me and said, "Bene."

"How come you don't talk to people?" I asked him in my fractured
Italian.

"No one speaks Italian here," he answered.

Luckily for us both, I had grown up in a community of two ethnic
groups—Jews and Italians.

This old fellow had been arrested during Prohibition for making
wine. He had come to America for a better life and wound up de
facto imprisoned in a mental hospital. This was during a time that the
commonwealth of Massachusetts had a very bad record with Italian
immigrants. The Saco-Vanzetti case had brought the plight of Italian

people in Massachusetts to public scrutiny (my grandfather had worked with them at the shoe factory in Brockton and had been a witness at the trial).

He wrote me long letters in Italian that my supervising psychiatrist (who spoke both Spanish and Italian) would translate for me. I tried hard to find this guy's family. The Italian consulate helped, but we were not able to locate any relatives. I set him up to go to an Italian nursing home. He was so happy. He thought about playing bocce again.

The day I went to pick him up for his placement, he died.

I was devastated. I had put a lot of work into this case to improve his life and right the wrong done to him by a blind and impassionate state system. I failed. Perhaps this feeling was based in a sense of childhood omnipotence to believe that I had enough control to right an egregious wrong. There is a Zen saying that "the boundary of your control ends at your skin." That was a hard lesson to learn. It was hard to accept this man's death before he could have some peace. Yet he had hope at the end of his life. Perhaps hope was the only salve I could offer.

I got drunk.

Then I started looking for a new job and promised myself that I would never work in a state mental hospital again. The system itself was abusive and absurd. After six months at that state hospital, I secured a traineeship in New Hampshire.

I have often wondered if my patient had thought that he might have been a victim of a series of accidents. Or did he just think that the system was unfair and abusive? I cannot ever ask him. I still mourn him to this day, and my experience with him made me an ardent worker on behalf of the obligations that we hold for those less fortunate or disenfranchised.

I have a feeling that this kind of ethical stance would have been appreciated by Heller and Vonnegut. In the end, their characters had to do what they considered as correct ... even if it was not consistent with the majority.

The problem in my life was to become humble about my decisions and not judgmental. Vonnegut appreciated that too. He ended *The Sirens of Titan* with a compassionate lie told to the protagonist of the story,

Malachai Constant, by his old friend Stony Stevenson. Malachai asks "I'm going to get into Paradise?" Stony tells him, "Don't' ask me why, old sport ... but somebody up there likes you." It was an unexpected ending, given the story's unfolding of the theme of accidental victims of life. Then again, reality is harsh, and sometimes we need to lie to get through it with caring and compassion.

The Talmud tells us that one is not only permitted to lie to a bride about her beauty, but we might be obligated to for the sake of compassion. Always tell the bride that she is beautiful. Even if she is not, she is beautiful on her special day. "One should always tell the truth, but you do not have to tell it all over the place."[25]

We all may indeed be victims of accidents, but sometimes ... just sometimes ... we might not have to remind people of that all over the place. Sometimes the relief of suffering requires a lie ... that someone up there cares about us.

Hope is an illusion we maintain as a survival mechanism. The nature of reality, being a set of probabilities and sometimes unrelated events, may be too hard a thought for us to live with. *The truth will make you free, but first it will make you miserable.* Yet, without hope, there is no life. It is hope that keeps us living and hope that keeps us loving. Even if I believe there is no one up there watching over us, I still hope that life can be better than it is today, that suffering can be reduced, and that well-being can increase for all living things.

Book 7

The Absurd Healer by Matthew P. Dumont, MD, 1972

Which one is the patient?[26]

In New Hampshire, where I worked as a mental health consultant (a fancy title for trainee), as I have related, I supported legalization of marijuana in 1969 in order to reduce crime and to increase the chemical purity control of the substance. This was somewhat strange, as I was not a marijuana smoker. That position was radical in 1969–70 and essentially got me thrown out of the community. Look where we are today! I was prophetic. But this unfortunate and stressful incident gave me the impetus to return to graduate school. The stress did not help my first marriage though. It just added to an already bad situation. We divorced in 1972 after three and a half years of marriage.

After graduating Springfield College with a master of education in counseling psychology in 1971, I secured a position as assistant director of intergroup relations for the city of Springfield, Massachusetts. I would later serve there as acting director. I was twenty-five years old, charged with assisting the desegregation of the Springfield School System as well as all of the legal and social issues to be improved on behalf of minority communities in Springfield. I also served as consultant representing the city to the Eighth Air Force Social Actions Program at Westover Air Force Base in Chicopee, right near Springfield. As with my previous positions, I undertook significant responsibilities at a young age. I had to work twice as hard as someone twice my age, just to be accepted as competent.

My background in mental health care served me well in my role in Springfield. While my work was communal in nature, I did keep my intense interest in psychodynamics and continued to read in that subject (such as *Ego and Instinct* by Barrett and Yankelovich, which was on my list of thirty-seven books). But I needed to come to grips with the theory and practice of community work, race relations, and minority relations in order to do my job well. Obviously, reading was a vehicle for this expansion of my intellectual activity. I read such books as Saul Alynski's *Rules for Radicals,* Eric Hoffer's books, *The Temper of Our Time, The True Believer,* and *The Ordeal of Change.* I read Gordon Alport's tome, *The Nature of Prejudice,* Stud Turkel's classic, *Working,* and Harry Katano's text *Race Relations.* I began carrying the *Constitution of the United States* with me. I got to teach intergroup relations as an adjunct instructor at Springfield College and began to develop my skills at this kind of college-level teaching.

In graduate school, I had held a position as a graduate teaching assistant in both social and behavioral psychology. Teaching intergroup relations as an adjunct instructor was a welcome professional addition to my teaching armamentarium. It would set the stage for later professional college teaching, which became a great skill and passion of mine. I love teaching, and I see my students appreciate me when I read their course evaluations and I go on the website RateYourProfessor.com.

In this new field for me of intergroup relations, I had to teach myself. I read voraciously and consulted frequently with my old professor, Walter English, EdD. Wally (as we all knew him) had held this position when the city decided to form an Office of Intergroup Relations and Human Relations Commission in 1968. He was African American and had served as a major in a segregated Army Air Corps in WWII. When I got the position, I went to tell him. He hugged me and said, "I don't know whether to laugh or cry for you." Over the next few years, Wally was the only person I could talk to who really knew what this job involved.

I was the first white man to hold a leadership role for that office. It probably did not hurt that I could pass for Hispanic, and many people congratulated the mayor for appointing the first Hispanic to lead the office. Little did they know that I was a white, middle-class Jew. When people discovered that, they were somewhat abashed. You can appear to others as they might want you to be. Besides, whatever I tried to say in Spanish had a Boston accent. It was a dead give away.

One book stood out to me among everything that I was studying to try to become really good at intergroup relations. That book was *The Absurd Healer* by Matthew P. Dumont, MD. The book was about community psychiatry, and it identified the community as the patient. I had already been exposed to public health and community psychiatry in Laconia, New Hampshire. I had read Gerald Caplan's *Principles of Preventive Psychiatry* while in traineeship. Caplan's consultative method reminded me of *Wasp* in that a single change agent could affect larger systems. Dumont reinforced this idea too. The idea of the community as the patient changed the trajectory of my professional interests.

I had already become familiar with Matthew P. Dumont's work through an unpublished paper of his called "What Is to Be Done?" about power and control in the governmental sector. I was impressed by his insight and great writing style. So, when I found his book on community psychiatry, I thought I had better read it. It was one of the most important books of my professional career.

Dumont's prognosis for our society was rather dark. His experiences as a community psychiatrist in New York City framed his thoughts. He was very clear that psychiatry needed to identify the community as the patient. It was the *system* that led people either into health or illness, in Dumont's reflections. By intervening in the systems that might produce illness, we stood half a chance at improving the lives of many people. He also criticized those practitioners who spent their time doing individual psychotherapy when the communities were so badly afflicted and it was the systems that needed remediation.

I saw that every day in my work in intergroup relations. Poverty, poor housing and nutrition, drugs and alcohol, lack of jobs, and lack of access to medical care all seemed to me to be just as important if not more so than a person's early childhood experiences and their intra-psychic mental mechanisms. I got it! It was, as Dumont suggested, the "confluence of systems"[27] that led to health or illness. Seeing people individually for counseling might be helpful, but changing systems would bring about the social changes that could spawn better lives for many. I was hooked. I became a "public healther" for the rest of my career.

The *Absurd Healer* is not a very long book. But it is jam-packed with truth statements. No other book on healthcare has had such an impact on my thinking about and professionally developing me to meet the challenges of social change. I will hearken back to *Wasp* at this point, because it was that book that stirred my awakening to the fact that a person could facilitate social change at all. I was committed to being a social change agent working on the systems that contributed to health—economics, housing, education, medical care, clean water and food, reduction in drug and alcohol abuse ...

Politically, this placed me in the Democratic camp. That is where I was from my upbringing anyway. My mother thought FDR was god! I am from Massachusetts and a Bostonian. I have to be a liberal Democrat by definition! Besides, I was a child of the sixties when socialism (or social welfarism) was in the air. What did the framers mean by "promote the general welfare" anyway?

I was excited about being an agent for change. I did not lose my concern for unconscious determinism, but I now had another framework to fit care into, and that was the community as a system. From that time forward, I would be concerned with Dumont's question, "Which one is the patient?"[28] in teaching psychologists, social workers, and even physicians. Not only "which one is the patient" but also what are the "confluence of systems" that lead to health or illness, and how can we affect those. It was at this point that I began to use the phrase "constellation of systems" that I have used ever since in teaching about community health.

During my time with the Department of Intergroup Relations for the city of Springfield, I was asked to lead our department's participation in the design and execution of desegregation busing, which was federally mandated. I am proud to say that our efforts yielded better results than the violence that accompanied busing in South Boston. That is because we did our homework well and because we had the concept of the city as patient.

Busing was latent with anxieties on all sides of the issue. Our department, in conjunction with the Springfield Urban League, conducted "A Study of Racial Attitudes" (locally published by the National Urban League of Springfield as a monograph) prior to designing a response to busing. We determined that the attitudes on all sides had to be taken into account if a busing program was to be successful and nonviolent. Everyone involved had to be involved in an active way.

We set up host families in each of the communities in which white and black families could serve as contact points for children being bused into those areas reciprocally. This proved to be a very well-appreciated strategy of creating an environment of mutual responsibility and obligations family to family. By involving everyone in the process, the process went off without major levels of violence. South Boston had not been so lucky. Desegregation experienced violence in that city.

That is not to say that there were not problems requiring resolution strategies. However, I do believe that the concept of the "community as patient" was indeed helpful to the proper execution of a social program of integration in a better way. I remain very proud of my contributions to this process, even if busing did not ultimately work in the long run. Overcoming racism, violence, and hatred is not a quick or easy process. However, it is clear to me that when one believes that everyone is the problem, that the community is the patient, then things can proceed in a more rational, expedient, and effective manner. Blaming the victim is never helpful, and focusing on one group rather than all groups is wrongly directed when trying to resolve societal issues.

And despite all this good work at racial integration, I received calls at home telling me that "the only good N----r is a dead N----r, and you will be one too." Intergroup relations work in the United States can be dangerous work. Death threats come with the territory. We are, after all, a country founded on racism against Native people, African people, ethnic non–Anglo Saxon people, and so forth. By serving black and brown and ethnic communities, I opened myself to danger.

Another aspect of our work at the Intergroup Relations Office was to work with the Migrant Farm Worker's Council to facilitate health care services to migrant tobacco farm workers in the Pioneer Valley of western Massachusetts. We formed a teaching program for community health workers. This could be dangerous work as well. I do not think that the employers were all that happy about people outside of their farms coming to care for crop workers. Any work on behalf of the disenfranchised in this country can carry risks with it.

It was also tough for me, as I did not speak Spanish. With the help of my administrative assistant who spoke Spanish, we put together a slide program using cartoons to augment Spanish captions through which I could teach health assessment. We thought it was innovative. It was well received in the Hispanic community.

What I find most interesting about this is how the entire project anticipated later involvements that I had with minority communities regarding healthcare delivery. When I was CEO of the Greater New Bedford Community Health Center, I was given a specific award by the regional Hispanic Recognition Committee and presented by the then treasurer of the United States for my work with Hispanic communities. In 2009, I became the chief operating officer for the (PACT) Prevention and Access to Care and Treatment Program at Brigham and Women's Hospital and Partners in Health (PIH), running a program for disenfranchised people throughout the country who had HIV/AIDS, multidrug-resistant TB, and diabetes. A significant number of our clients were of Hispanic origin or background.

Despite all of this work with Hispanic communities, I never did get to learn Spanish other than *hola*. Boston accents and Spanish do not work well together.

So, there is Matthew P. Dumont sitting on my bookshelf, always reminding me to consider the entire system, the confluence of systems,[29] and what I call the constellation of systems that come together to make us well or ill. The community is the patient.

This model served me well when I went to work in the addictions field at Rutland Heights Hospital as well. How can we possibly believe that we can work on individuals and return them to the very family and community systems that made them sick in the first place and then expect them (patients) to recover and not to relapse? If you did not work on the system, then all of the individual work in the world will have a low probability of success. To quote Dumont, "And in the cities, psychiatrists are doing little more than psychotherapy."[30]

As for my social life in 1972, I met my wife Debbie Tomchik at work in Springfield. She was a student from Elmira College doing an internship with our department's anthropologist on Hispanic demographics. She accompanied me on a business trip to UMass Amherst. I fell in love within hours. We had lunch at Wiggins Tavern in Northampton and went to see the *Canterbury Tales* at UMass. We drove and talked and drove and talked. Work seemed very far away. I felt feverish and compelled to be with Debbie all of the time. We did not return for three days, at which time I proposed. Two weeks after that, she accepted. *This was the most exciting time of my life* outside of having our three children. To date at the time of this writing, we have been married for forty-seven years.

Of course, once we became a couple, one of us had to quit. The department director was able to work it out so that Debbie could finish her internship without any supervisory relationship to myself. The next months were dramatic for her, as she changed schools, converted to Judaism, and prepared for a wedding. Being the only girl in her nuclear family, this was a big event. Since it was my second marriage, there were obvious fears involved. But I got the blessing of her parents and her uncles (a mother's brothers are very important in a Greek family).

Our wedding was itself an exercise in intergroup relations, with my Russian Jewish grandmother singing songs with the Polish side of the family at their table and the Greek side of Debbie's family dancing in the opposite direction of the Jews dancing the Hora. We honeymooned in

Montreal in January, for which Debbie never forgave me until we went to Jamaica for a warm vacation years later!

In early 1974, my new wife, Debbie, and I moved to Washington, DC, where I started a doctoral program in management science. Debbie had left Elmira College and transferred to Springfield College when we married. She would complete her degree during our time in DC. But as for me, the school I went to found itself in some serious problems affecting its viability, and we left to come home to Springfield, Massachusetts, in November 1974. I had been working on my dissertation. These events would be the first in a series of significant stressors on us over our years of marriage.

Debbie and my engagement picture in 1972

I do have to say that the education I received in Washington was very good, and I learned a lot about management from some outstanding teachers. Since I had determined that management was where I was going anyway, a doctorate in management science made sense. Not being able to complete this was a big body blow. I would rather run organizations that serve as a cog in them. I was concerned about leadership and being a change agent from the top and not from the bottom. Ego, I suppose, was at work here, as were my needs for power and control. But I also had leadership skills that had been proven in my work in the air force and in Springfield, and I had a serious interest in using them to the benefit of others. I have always credited the US Air Force with first teaching me administration. I did have an affinity for bureaucracy.

Back in Springfield, with Debbie pregnant and twenty-six cents in our pockets, we depended on "Al Forman's welfare system" until I could get a job. We lived in a house that Debbie's cousin was selling until we could get our own apartment in Oxford, Massachusetts. In January 1975, I became the assistant director of the Public Inebriate Program at the Rutland Heights Hospital run by the MA Department of Public Health and Catholic Charities. This job would lead me to some major accomplishments and life events over the next almost fifteen years.

I took the job on January 2, 1975, and moved into an apartment in Oxford, Massachusetts, leaving Deb back in Springfield to wrap up our life there. She was pregnant with our first child. This would become a pattern in our lives of me moving away for work first and then Deb wrapping up our lives and following.

I moved with minimal possessions, which included a sleeping bag, pillow, cup, pot, knife, fork and spoon, a lamp, the five books of Moses, and a short Samurai sword. That was it besides some clothing. I would work and then return to the empty apartment until Deb joined me a couple of months later. It was a hard routine for two newlyweds. Despite the paucity of my possessions, I never slept better. There is something to be said for Buddhist nonattachment and simplicity.

At Rutland Heights Hospital (RHH), I came under the leadership of Ender K. Brunner, MD. Dr. Brunner, in my opinion, was one of the great public health leaders in Massachusetts. His philosophy of public health and healthcare was entirely consistent with what I had learned in my work in Springfield and through my studying both Gerald Caplan's and Matthew P. Dumont's works.

Dr. Brunner knew every one of the 265 patients at RHH by name. He was someone to emulate as a healthcare provider. He was demanding but fair. Like other mentors I was fortunate enough to have had in my life, he believed in me and took an interest in my development. It was he who directed me to become a member of the American College of Healthcare Executives and to pursue my license in psychology. He was a physician administrator who encouraged me to combine my healthcare experience with public health and leadership to the benefit of society. I owe Dr. Brunner a lot.

Our first son was born on Mother's Day 1975. We were living in Oxford, Massachusetts, but drove into Springfield to have him. The day was spectacularly beautiful, and Debbie's contractions seemed to stop during our ride. The labor restarted in the hospital and was not fun. I took a valium that was meant for Debbie! Debbie's head spun around like Linda Blair in the *Exorcist,* and she made noises I never thought could come out of a human being. And then, this perfect little man came into the world, forty-five years ago at this writing.

In 1977, we bought our first house in Worcester, and in 1978, we had our second son. Life was awfully busy in those days. I followed Dr. Brunner's advice and pursued both joining the American College of Healthcare Executives and getting my psychology license, which required studying for a national board exam.

I passed the board exam, got my psychology license in November 1978, and began a private practice in December of that year. I was one of only a few master-level psychologists allowed to take the exam, which normally required a PhD. My father doubted I would pass but was very proud when I did. He was sure that a master-level person would either not pass or not be allowed to become licensed. Passing was indeed quite an accomplishment for me. I was proud that my father was proud.

My DBA (doing business as) was Stuart I. Forman Associates, as I did not yet have a doctorate in 1978. I practiced under that DBA title until 1990 when I became the CEO of the Greater New Bedford

Community Health Center in New Bedford, Massachusetts, and closed my practice. I became director of psychological services at Rutland Heights Hospital when I got my license in psychology in 1978.

After I received my Massachusetts license to practice psychology, I was accepted into a nontraditional PhD program through the California-state-licensed (sans regional accreditation) graduate program, double majoring in psychology and health administration at Columbia Pacific University (CPU). I earned the degree in November, 1979. Like my advanced standing in my BS and MEd programs, I received advanced standing based on my experience, education, and training. Since I had passed the national boards in psychology, that was credited as evidence of a comprehensive exam in that specific discipline. I entered the program at the doctoral project level.

For those who attended licensed nontraditional programs in the 1970s, the currency of such degree programs could pose an issue in various circumstances as the decades went on. I was always obsessively concerned with being ethical in these respects and diligent about providing full disclosure to avoid such issues. This turned out to be far less of a problem for colleagues and employers than it was for me over the course of my career. It did not interfere with my professions or academic appointments. While I was circumspect about the use of the degree, it did pose quite a bit of obsessive consternation for me. I was upset when CPU closed twenty years later.

Nontraditional programs can be vehicles for those at work and with familial responsibilities. Today, distance programs and online programs are common but pose their own issues for students, teachers, and the public. My master of science in Jewish studies at Spertus College (which I earned in 2008) was a hybrid program combining both on-site and distance learning. While fully regionally accredited, it still is somewhat of a nontraditional program. I could never have undertaken that degree while working. And that is exactly what I did in both 1979 (PhD) and 2005 (MSJS). I was fortunate to have had the opportunity of distance learning available to me as a working person.

Our second son was born in 1978 and our third son was born in

1980. Life was very full both personally and professionally. I was now working three jobs to make a living for our new family of five. I worked at the hospital, had a private practice, and did organizational consulting.

On Thanksgiving Day 1980, my father had a massive heart attack and died at our family home in Newton, Massachusetts. I said Kaddish for him three times a day for the prescribed eleven months. I think it took me about five years just to wake up from his death. He missed everything about his grandchildren, and I am sorry for that for him. I loved my father and respected him as an ethical man despite his verbal abusiveness. It was easy to be his friend but hard to be his son. I regret that he never told me that he loved me in words. That was a hole that could not be filled.

As if all of this was not enough on my busy plate, I also was studying martial arts in the Kenpo and Jujitsu systems. My supervisor and one of my colleagues were both involved in these arts. My supervisor was a new student, and my colleague was a black belt. My colleague was one of the best martial artists I have known. Through my association with these two friends and their encouragement, I began my training. I earned my brown belt in Kenpo and Jujitsu in 1977 and a black belt in kickboxing in 1979.

I had no money, of course, being a public servant. So, I took the job as chief instructor for the Karate Club at our local Jewish community center. Without the money from that job, I would not have been able to keep my practice open until my patient load increased and I had developed a cash flow.

Except for the support of my wife, I have no idea how I undertook so much during those years or accomplished what I did. I do know that I became very fond of Oriental philosophy and meditation through this period of martial arts training and association with my two friends. That is how I came back to the *Tao Te Ching* and expanded my interests into Zen. Being a child of the 1960s, I am somewhat surprised that I did not delve into Zen in more depth in college. It really was martial arts training that opened Zenism to me.

Debbie was busy with our three sons in those days. She was so busy that it seems to me that in later life, that period of time might be a blur to her. Her involvement was home and kids and trying to make ends meet on my public servant's salary. Deb got her real estate license and later her appraiser's license. She worked at those professions and enjoyed them.

Debbie has been the Aeyshes Chayal ("The Woman of Valor") who is praised in song on Shabbat. Having taken my mother into our home to care for her with her disease of dementia for six years, Debbie applied for sainthood. Caring for my mother and raising three boys with me out trying to make a living could make her cranky. The burden fell on her, and it was true that my work affected my availability at home. This placed significant stress on our family.

My mother remained with us for six years before we had to put her into a nursing home because of the intensity of her care. She stayed at the New Bedford Convalescent home for another seven years before she died. At the same time, Auntie Rae developed bladder cancer in Florida. Her illness required us to travel to Florida to supervise her care and estate. I cared for my aunt as if she was my second mother, which she was to a large extent. She died in 2006. My mother died in 2008.

I could not have taken care of my mother and Auntie Rae without Debbie. My mother used to say that she did not have a daughter-in-law, but she had a daughter (Debbie). Still, the stress was real.

I certainly did not have familial analogues for raising three boys. I never had siblings. I did have a father whose model for a working person was to be out of the home most of the day. In some ways at work, I modeled my father. My boys complained about this in later life, only to replicate it themselves in adult life. This is what Murray Bowen called multigenerational differentiation of self. It is hard to break long-term patterns of family behavior.

I have seen my sons repeat this multigenerational pattern of frenetic work resulting in less availability at home. It is very stressful on families and on marriages. My father did it. I did it. My sons appear to me to do it. And I regret the pattern.

Balancing work, education, and family life responsibilities is not easy. Yet, despite my best efforts, I still heard dissatisfaction with my role at home. I heard it both verbally and behaviorally. While it might be worse for working women, I assure you that it is not fun for men. One learns to carry a significant degree of guilt for leading such a life.

Martial arts was both a help and a hindrance to salving my guilt. On the one hand, it helped with the Buddhist concept of nonattachment. On the other hand, I was at dojo (martial arts school) three times a week. Buddhism works best if you are a monk, I think.

My impressions from *The Absurd Healer* were life determinative. You cannot separate yourself from other people in a family, at work, or in society at large. *It is connectedness that frames health and not disconnectedness.* And it was my community that helped me navigate the stressors of life.

In trying to answer the question I have about my own resiliency in light of the many stressors I have discussed above, it seems to me that the single most important variable toward health has been my own connectedness in the web of human experiences. Having friends, colleagues, family, and a religious community have all contributed to my ability to deal with stress. These have helped me in dark times and times when my OCD was most upsetting. These have helped me to deal with a number of life-threatening illnesses.

There is nothing more important to human health than a community. There has been little more important to me than having a community around me. I can talk to myself, but that is far less useful. I can talk to my dogs, but they can only offer their behavioral love (read appendix C).

This might be Dumont's most important lesson. It is not the "economy stupid"[31]; it is the community that is most important!

A final note from understanding Dumont: the number one concomitant of illness in the United States is poverty, and the second concomitant is racism. Combating poverty and racism are not things that can be accomplished on an individual-by-individual basis. It can only be accomplished by the community as a whole group of people.

Another huge issue in health and illness is isolation. Neither my mother nor my aunt would have survived as long or as well as they did without our assistance. It was not easy. It was a mitzvah.

We cannot be alone in life.

Zen in the Martial Arts by Joe Hyams, 1980

When you seek it, you cannot find it.[32]

I found one book that seemed an excellent summary of Zen. That book is *Zen in the Martial Arts* by Joe Hyams. That summary of Zen (and Tao) made it to my list of most important books. I found this book the year after I got my black belt.

Zen in the Martial Arts is a very short but profound book. In fact, I seem to like short but profound books versus six-hundred-page tomes. It summarizes in readable form the philosophies behind the martial arts and provides a path for Zen practice without the need to convert to Buddhism. The practices and stories can be melded into one's current Western practices only with some effort. It is also good, like in any discipline, to have a teacher. Reading a book is ultimately insufficient. You have to practice and experience what you learned. Teachers and practice … how profound!

Zenism has had an appeal way beyond the arts in Western society. To some extent, it has been an integral part of the American 1960–70s culture. It was not surprising to me, then, that some American Jewish people also tried to incorporate Zenism into Judaism. *The Jew in the Lotus* by Roger Kamenetz helped to articulate some of the Jewish-Buddhist interface. The book describes the meeting of the Dalai Lama with a group of Jewish rabbis led by Rabbi Zalman Shachter Shalomi. Rabbi Schachter has been the leader of a spiritual movement within Judaism to claim or reclaim Jewish spirituality. The interface between spiritual disciplines East and West has been an area of exploration for many people's interests.

Thus, there exists a movement within Judaism called "JuBus" or Jewish Buddhists. The disciplines are sometimes not as far from each other as one might think. Being a martial artist and an orthopraxis Jew (at the time) helped me to understand this movement and to feel somewhat comfortable with combining these two disciplines.

Of course, in terms of Chinese religions, one must be clear that there are gods within those traditions. Buddhism had its beginning in India and in Hinduism, where there are many gods. Certainly, there are those who would contend that Buddhism is an atheistic religion because it does not postulate a creator deity. In Buddhist tradition, the universe is eternal. If it is eternal, then one does not need a creator deity. And yet, like Hinduism and classical Chinese religion, Buddhism has many gods. So is it atheistic, monotheistic, or polytheistic? This did concern me as a monotheist Jew.

There are some who contend that Hinduism is in fact a monotheistic tradition. All gods in the Hindu pantheon are avatars of Brahman. So, it is Brahman who is the one god. How does this differ from a primitive Judaism that has an angelology and Celestial Retinue in which an angel is a messenger of the One God and delivers one message or fulfills one purpose determined by God? Is a Celestial Retinue very much different from the various representations of a single deity?

These are deep and important religio-philosophical/theological issues that are beyond the scope of this essay. Yet I think it is important to notice the similarities and differences between Taoism, Zen Buddhism, and Judaism to be able to understand the waters I had to navigate in my spiritual quest. It was the end of that quest that I was concerned about in a rapprochement between Western and Eastern disciplines. Ultimately, the goals seemed similar while the paths had different disciplines; the goals were the reduction of suffering and increase of well-being of all living things. That is my own generalization. Actually, the goal in Taoism is noninterference; the goal in Zen is to attain emptiness of the mind as a path to nonattachment; and the goal of Judaism centers around themes of exile and return and the establishment of social justice.

The ultimate goal of the reduction of suffering and the increase of well-being was my spiritual quest, whether I knew it at the time or not. Indeed, during these days up until the turn of the twenty-first century, my quest focused on Judaism and Judaic practice while interweaving Taoist and Zen practices into that matrix. Of course, my quest led to my children's confusions about Judaism. I am clear in my own mind that each discipline has major wisdom to offer. But they are not all the same no matter how much JuBus (Jewish Buddhists) want them to be the same.

Judaism is a difficult practice. "Schwer sein eine Yid" (It is hard to be a Jew) goes the Yiddish expression on the subject. That is true. Jewish practice has many dos and don'ts called "Ta'aseh" and "Lo Ta'aseh" respectively. The rigidity of practice in the Orthodox world can lead one out of the secular world. That can be very confusing, especially for young people. The end results of this for my children are that I produced one Jewish agnostic, one JuBu Zenist, and one Jewish atheist.

Parents can learn from their children. As my knowledge in my quest grew, I had more appreciation for my sons' positions on religion. I did not like it, but I grew to have an understanding of it and how my quest may have affected them. I wish I had been less confused during the early years of my children's lives. It might have been easier for them.

My middle son is a trained martial artist and values the Tao and Zen about as much as I do. I am happy about that. But combining Eastern and Western traditions is not easy. Even combining Western traditions is not easy. For example, three-quarters of our family are intermarried, including Debbie's and my family. One of our children's family has Christmas (without the tree and trappings but traditions of gathering and gift giving). The other two have had Christmas trees, although not for the celebration of Jesus but more for secular purposes. Even so ... this is the general Jewish American parent's dilemma. Many of our friends' families are similar. Combining traditions can be a challenge, whether East and West or just within a single pluralistic society.

All of my sons are busy with work and family. Like most people of their generation, spirituality is not primary on their lists of concerns. I get it. I had a hectic life as well. But I was always conflicted within my quest for the spiritual and my relationship to the Jewish people going all the way back to my relationship with my maternal grandfather. It was only as an adult that I came to understand my grandparents' Zionism and cultural Judaism as their primary motivations and not their spiritual affinity to a radical monotheism. As I stated above, my parents were cultural Jews rather than religious Jews, with my mother being a declared agnostic, my aunt being an atheist (kind of), and my father never discussing the matter.

One solution to combining various differing traditions is to adopt the traditions of the majority, but as the Holocaust has shown us, "You can run, but you can't hide."[33] You might actually be able to combine Oriental and Occidental societies faster than Eastern European Jewish and Christian societies.

My spiritual quest did include valuing Taoism, Buddhism, and Zen Buddhism. But first and foremost, I valued Judaism and the Jewish people. As our family grew and marriages occurred (including my own), intermarriage was prominent. How does one honor another person's traditions while being devoted to one's own? Christmas poses a huge social issue in this regard. I will deal with this in more detail later on. Suffice it to say that whether one is trying to spiritually combine Eastern and Western thought or Christian and Jewish traditions, it ain't an easy task.

Back to martial arts and Zenism. In 1987, our martial arts group dispersed, each member going on to other things and locations in life. You cannot be a rogue martial artist … or an injured one. I injured my back when I was forty years old, chopping wood for our Franklin stove that we heated our home with. I could not kick again.

I had to come to grips with the fact that I was a non-practicing martial artist. I did take up Tai Chi for a year. Joe Hyams's book gave me an increased avenue to learn from the arts, even if I was unable to fight. Zen is about living. Its wisdom is valuable no matter what you are doing in life. I enjoyed kickboxing at full contact, but my injuries set me on a different path.

I mentioned before that had I not been a martial artist and student of Oriental philosophy, getting through my father's death in 1980 would have been much more difficult. Oh yes, saying Kaddish and observing the Jewish mourning ritual were eminently helpful, but the concept of just letting things take their course, of not pushing the world to be as I wanted it to be and having an empty mind were Zen concepts that helped with the loss.

On reflection, taking up martial arts was a way to deal with my childhood insecurities around frailness. I had Wolff-Parkinson-White cardiac syndrome, which limited my activities as a young person. I also had developed asthma (who knew it was related to my allergies to our cat, Lao?). And, finally, I had a lot of anger to express: anger at my father's rages; anger at my mother's ineffectiveness in saving me from that tyranny; anger at myself for what I perceived as underperformance. I had a lot to kick and punch out. Sometime after my father died, I stopped kicking and punching. The reader can assess the psychodynamics behind that.

The 1980s, after my father's death, were frenetic for me. I opened a second office in Springfield as well as Worcester. I was consulting and teaching all over the commonwealth. I was working as director of psychological services at Rutland Heights Hospital (RHH),where I had developed the Center for Alcohol and Substance Abuse Disorders (CASAD). In 1986, I began teaching at the University of Massachusetts Medical School (RHH) and received appointment as assistant professor of family and community medicine in 1987. In 1986, I also began work that would bring about the creation of the commonwealth of Massachusetts's Bradford R. Burn Post-Traumatic Stress Disorders Unit (for combat Vietnam veterans) at RHH. I helped to design and open the Massachusetts Second DUI Offenders Program at Rutland Heights Hospital and the neurobehavioral program at Tewksbury Hospital. I helped to create an adolescent drug treatment program at Rutland Heights Hospital. I published a major research piece on addiction curriculum in medical education with my teaching colleague at UMMS and an article on our PTSD program with the acting commissioner of public health. In 1987, I received the highest award in public service in Massachusetts from Governor Michael S. Dukakis, the Manual Carballo Governor's Award for Excellence in Public Service.

To add sauce to the goose, our son's bar mitzvahs occurred from 1988 through 1993. Our move to southeastern Massachusetts occurred in 1995. Busy, busy, busy.

I left public service in 1988 to become the associate director of human services for the Hubbard Regional Hospital in Webster, Massachusetts. I had spent fourteen years of my life at RHH. Most of that time was developing and running programming as well as fighting the commonwealth to keep the hospital open. In 1989, it was closed. I attended the closing ceremony, and the loss was devastating for me.

With all of this and a family of three boys to feed and father, I wound up in a psychiatrist's office in 1987 with severe anxiety. Zen and psychiatry helped me get better. But I was one overwhelmed, hurting puppy. Even recognitions can be stressful. My family and I paid a price for my level of work and overachievement.

I do have a final question about Zen. How could a culture that integrated Zen Buddhism into it have committed atrocities in China, Korea, and Southeast Asia, raped Nanking, and started WWII in the Pacific? *Zen in the Martial Arts* does not provide an answer to this question. But then again, how did the culture that produced the likes of Goethe, Bach, and Beethoven create the Holocaust? I have not been able to fully come to grips with the disconnects in these very important questions. What kind of evolutionary disconnect could be behind these dilemmas? I do not know the answer.

So, let me not romanticize or over-evaluate Zen. Let me keep the questions open and unresolved.

Life is complicated and confusing.

Zen in the Martial Arts taught me the value of no mind, of acceptance, and of how hard those things really are to acquire. Zen is interesting though because you cannot strive toward anything, like Tao. You can only become awake. This is entirely contradictory to the striving theme of this book.

"When you seek it, you cannot find it." This is one of the wisdom statements in Hyams's book. I value that. I just have not been very good at *being* that.

A Brief History of Time: From the Big Bang to Black Holes by Stephen Hawking, 1988

For then we would know the mind of god.[34]

Warning: This chapter discusses physics and might seem somewhat dry. But physics is so important to me and my understanding of the way the world works that I cannot leave it out.

But if you do struggle through my writing style in this chapter, you will find that there is plenty to catch your fancy further on. Understanding me is both an intellectual and an affective project.

It could be that my intellectualizing, as evidenced in my love of physics, is a defense mechanism. It is hard to find other people to talk to who appreciate intellectual play. Usually, I only find this in academia. But I do like intellectual play.

The first elective course I took in my graduate program in Jewish studies was called The Heavens. It studied physics from Aristotle through string theory and their effects on Jewish theology. It was the best course I have ever taken. That summarizes where my interests lie.

In1988, Stephen Hawking published *A Brief History of Time*. It sold thirty million copies worldwide. Auntie Rae bought it for me for my birthday. I do not know of another physicist who enjoyed this level of notoriety other than Sir Isaac Newton and Albert Einstein. What

Hawking did was to make physics and its fundamental philosophical questions available to the nonphysics, nonmathematical world. This was a great accomplishment that enriched so many people's lives. It enriched my life, and I feel that I would be neglectful if I did not cite Hawking's works as influential on me.

A Brief History of Time was a segue for me to other major philosophical and scientific concerns. These were alluded to in *A Brief History of Time* and expanded upon in Hawking's later books, such as his book *The Grand Design* with Leonard Mlodinow. *A Brief History of Time* helped the non-physics world appreciate the two great pillars of physics: general relativity and quantum mechanics. It helped to get some sense of why Einstein's work was of such magnitude and overturned the entire worldview of Sir Isaac Newton.

Without dwelling on formulas, Hawking introduced readers to the concept of space-time and the equivalency between energy and matter ($E=mc^2$). He explained the concepts of matter warping space-time to generate gravity and space-time telling matter how to move. He introduced the concepts of quantum superposition and entanglement to the lay public. He introduced us to the two great pillars of physics, being relativity for the physics of the very large and quantum physics for the physics of the very small. These are not easy concepts. But to become familiar with them even in passing is to enhance one's world.

Hawking also alluded to things that he further articulated in later writings, such as *The Grand Design*. Two important items for me include "logical positivism" and "model dependent reality." *These are concepts I had been looking for my entire life!* In the first case of positivism, to understand the world without metaphysics through verification and/or falsification of statements is crucial to those of us who value science and the scientific method. This was the concept underlying the School of Logical Positivism created by the Vienna Circle in Austria in the 1920–30s by people like Rudolph Carnap, Moritz Schlicht, and others.[35]If a statement is not falsifiable (Karl Popper) or verifiable (A.J. Ayer), then it is not meaningful within the scientific realm. Perhaps it might have meaning metaphysically, but metaphysics does not necessarily depend on proof and material evidence.

Anyone can have a belief. Beliefs, by definition, do not necessitate empirical proofs. One could believe that the world is flat, but without proof, that statement is probably meaningless in any practical sense. Growing up with an aunt who worked at MIT led me to a scientific appreciation of the world and how it worked. That probably frustrated my spiritual questing over my lifetime. So, understanding positivism was really important for me. It also had an effect on my religious understandings, as the reader will see in the section that follows.

Of course, through intensive study, I found that I might not be a full logical positivist but rather a "post-positivist," based on Kurt Gödel's postulate that not all truths can be proved true and that no system can prove itself. If that (the incompleteness theorem) really is the case, and Heisenberg's uncertainty principle is true, then verification and falsification may be ultimately limited in terms of truth statements. This would leave us in a condition of ultimate uncertainty. We can tell how things probably are but not how they definitively are.

For me, the three legs of the modern stance on skepticism include the Heisenberg uncertainty principle, Schrodinger's cat thought experiment, and Gödel's incompleteness theorem. The stool of modern skepticism, dating itself as a philosophical tradition all the way back to Pyrrho in ancient Greece, rests on these three people and their findings. In the case of the uncertainty principle, we are shown that we cannot know definitively the position and momentum of a particle at the same time. We can only know these within parameters of probabilities. In the second case of Schrodinger's cat thought experiment, we cannot know with a certainty whether the cat is alive or dead until it is observed, at which point both wave functions of *alive* and *dead* collapse into a single wave function of either alive or dead.

The process of observation changes the event itself. Observation does not make the observed as we wish to see it. It only collapses the wave functions into a single wave function. So, it is not the case that observation *determines* the outcome of what is being observed. Observation only *changes* the probable into something distinctly observable. Quantum mechanics is counterintuitive fields that can make us feel uncomfortable. Things may only exist when they come into relation to something else. To exist might mean that something can be measured. So this leaves us with a rather slushy universe.

I would continue this discussion using the issue of superposition and quantum entanglement. However, this issue is so spooky (to use Einstein's word) that I am afraid I might get entangled in trying to explain how two particles can have the exact same characteristics even if separated by great distance. This implies that space-time itself might be illusionary. I will leave this part of the discussion to those more competent than I to explain it.

Finally, and to repeat, the incompleteness theorem tells us that we cannot prove all truths as true and that no system can prove itself. In other words, we cannot know anything at 100 percent degree of certainty but only within the parameters of probabilities. Physics has led the way to the philosophical position taken twenty-five centuries ago, that we should be skeptical because we cannot know everything definitively at a 100 percent degree of confidence.

Human beings are essentially hunting animals and do not like uncertainty. You cannot hunt if you are not certain as to where the prey you are hunting is located. Yet, even back to the Talmudic period, the great sages of Judaism postulated that some truth cannot be proved and came up with the principle of "Tayku" or "there is no answer." This can keep one humble about knowledge, just as Kurt Gödel's incompleteness theorem showed that one cannot prove all truths.

As a side note, I spent much of the late eighties and nineties studying Talmud. After a total of twenty years of study, I had completed eight major tractates and a number of minor tractates. From this writer's understanding, that is a lot. The Talmud is so extensive that if you studied one page a day, it would take you seven years to complete it.

The sages of the Talmud had obsessive-compulsive disorder to a certain extent. I have that malady myself. Nothing escaped their review in depth. Two very important Talmudic principles that I appreciated as a scientist were the concept above of Tayku (there is no answer) and the concept of *aeyleh v' aeyleh*, or "this and this are true." That is clearly not Aristotelian thought processes. They are not categorical finalities. They are concepts without which quantum physics could not exist, and modern physics would fall apart.

So, at this point in my life, I was trying to interweave Taoism, Zen Buddhism, Judaism, and physics. It is interesting to be a positivist and a spiritual person at the same time. No wonder my family and I were confused! My wife criticizes this effort, stating that positivism is devoid of spirituality. I disagree. I think that physics gives one a *sense of awe* in the universe, and what is awe if not the beginnings of spirituality?

Some of this quest led to secularism and some to a general understanding and acceptance of uncertainty. Understanding Heisenberg's uncertainty principle, Schrodinger's cat thought experiment, and Gödel's incompleteness theorem might lead one to model dependent reality and to be a post-positivist who is humble about the extent of knowledge we can acquire.

To be a real secularist, one only needs to add to these matters Darwin's evolutionary theory, psychoanalytic theory, and the documentary hypothesis (or higher text criticism) of the Bible. It would probably be wrong of me not to include the theodicy of the post-Holocaust era and existentialism, as it appreciates the absurd. And, voila, there you have it ... *modern secularism* and the venerable philosophical tradition dating from Pyrrho of *skepticism* supported on an eight-legged sofa. These all swirled around my head along with Zenism, Judaism, and logical positivism. I am sure this drove my family and friends nuts.

In each of the cases supporting secularism, the need for a creator deity is not necessary. That does not mean that one must become an atheist. It only means that one might wish to redefine what they mean by the word *god*. The idea of a creator deity thatintervenes in the laws of physics on behalf of certain people seems intellectually disingenuous. Couldn't we just propose that what we mean by the word *god* is our awe of the process through which the universe works? Couldn't we just agree to be in awe of the *verb* god and not the *noun* god? That would make things so much simpler and take god off the hook for the theodicy question.

Einstein understood the concept of god in a similar way to Spinoza in that he did not attribute intervention in the affairs of people to a god. God set up the rules of the universe, and off it went. This is not far from the deism of the American founding fathers and the Enlightenment. None of this meant that these great thinkers were not in awe of the universe. It did mean that divine intervention could not be squared with the concept of evil.

These all were weaving their way around one another in my quest for truth and my quest for spirituality. One seemed to complement the other but eluded my ability to define clearly a path for myself. Whatever path I had chosen, Zenism and Taoism had more resonance for my family than the religion of the Jewish people. It was the Tao that came to be the central spiritual book in my family and not the Torah of Moses. While this may be sad, it is the way things seemed to be on the East and West Coasts of the US in the mid to late twentieth century.

I already noted how physics has been rather a hobby of mine since college. That is true. But just like being a rogue martial artist and a rogue Jew and a rogue philosopher, you cannot just do these things alone. You need other people of like-mindedness. And if you are not in an academic community, this is tough. I was not within such a community. I had my books but few to talk with about these matters of importance to me, though clearly not to other "normal" people. This was a lonely place to be. But I was not a stranger to intellectual loneliness.

As an only child, I knew how all of this felt from childhood. As an intellectual, I knew that this path was lonely. Interestingly, I hated to be alone. That was how I met my wife. I hated driving alone. I always sought company. She agreed to go with me on a business trip from Springfield to Amherst. And the rest, as they say, is history.

It was not until much later in my life that I learned to be alone. That was when I had to live in Pennsylvania when I was the CEO for the Jewish Community Alliance of Northeastern Pennsylvania in 2016–2017. Deb had to stay back to sell our condo and then moved in with our middle son's family before we bought our home in New York. I took an apartment in Wilkes-Barre, Pennsylvania, and came home on weekends. I was alone, but I had my work and my books.

My books were my friends. I promised myself that I would only take one hundred books to Pennsylvania, where I would be for one to two years. I took two hundred and fifty. Well, that is what happened with this experiment. I was supposed to pick twelve; I picked thirty-seven and wound up with a total of fourteen. I am verbose. That experience in Pennsylvania helped me be alone. Today, as a retired person, I am alone a lot, and it is okay.

I still proceeded on a quest for a Judaism I could live with. I was and am still devoted to the Jewish people and their magnificent contributions to the human experiment. In these respects, I am continuously studying, learning, and finding ways to put this knowledge to good use.

In summary, here are some of my life conclusions by the time I entered middle age:

1. Life is absurd.
2. Despite the absurdity, one must go on.
3. Learning is key to developing a sense of understanding of oneself and one's place in this absurd universe.
4. The universe is counterintuitive.
5. It is a talent, if not an art, to be able to live with the absurd, uncertainty, and counter-intuition and to still find purpose and meaning.
6. We are deluded to believe that we have enough agency to remake the laws of physics to our own purposes.
7. The universe unfolds itself according to its unfolding and not according to our wishes.
8. The truth will make you free, but first it will make you miserable.
9. You should always tell the truth, but you do not have to tell it all over the place.
10. Even in an unpredictable and often absurd universe, there is value in the past, in family, in reducing suffering and increasing

well-being in the here and now rather than spending inordinate time worrying about an undeterminable future or unproven afterlife.

11. We need to be very humble about our predictions.

12. We need to be healthily skeptical because we can never know anything at 100 percent degree of confidence.

Is there a single conclusion to my learning from Hawking's book? Yes. I am humbled before the universe.

13. Even at their best, marriage and family life are hard work and are not for the faint of heart.

14. One should be ethical but not to the point of immobilization. Get the best advice you can and make an informed decision based on that. Then move forward.

15. Living in society, we all have social obligations and responsibilities.

Here is my takeaway from *A Brief History of Time*: the universe is awesome and complicated. *We can strive to understand the universe but only with humility as to the boundaries of our own understanding.*

Book 10

Yosl Rakover Talks to God
by Zvi Kolitz, 1988

I die at peace, but not pacified, conquered and beaten
but not enslaved, bitter but not disappointed, a believer
but not a supplicant, a lover of God but not His blind
Amen-sayer.[36]

The 2013 Pew study on Jewish demographics and attitudes showed that
some 78 percent of the survey's respondents said that remembering the
Holocaust was important to being Jewish.[37] It is important to being
human, let alone being Jewish.

What does "remembering the Holocaust" mean? This is similar to
asking the question, "What does being Jewish mean?" There are many
answers by the many people concerned with this issue. (See the Pearl
family's book, *I Am Jewish,* commemorating Daniel Pearl's last words
before the Taliban decapitated him.)[38]For some, remembering the horror
and abuse is important, especially if you are a survivor. For others,
understanding the process of how the Holocaust happened is important.
For still others, there is the matter of the meaning of the Holocaust to
the issues of faith and theodicy. I, personally, am concerned with all of
the above. But I have one other serious concern as a Jew; I do not want
the Holocaust to define who I am as a Jew or as a person. That would
mean that Hitler won.

After the war, a Jewish philosopher, Emile Fachenheim, set forth the 614th Commandment (there are 613 Commandments in the Torah). That 614th Commandment was not to grant Adolf Hitler a posthumous victory.[39] These are profound words with significant if not existential meaning. I will come back to this issue a bit later when discussing assimilation.

Rabbi Baruch Goldstein, my friend and mentor, survived both Birkenau and Auschwitz. He lost his entire family in the war and recorded his experiences in his book, *For Decades I Kept Silent*. The rabbi was also a man of deep faith, and his book explored the issue of his maintenance of his faith after the Holocaust. In other words, a part of his book dealt with trauma, and a part of his book dealt with theodicy. Rabbi Goldstein never lost his faith and became a rabbi after his experiences in the camps. Although I had a hard time understanding such faith, my regular walks with the rabbi helped me to understand him and his beliefs.

I remember one year in which I was distraught by work and had decided to quit. The president of our health system and my friend recommended that I go away on personal retreat before making any momentous decisions. Before I left, I stopped by to see Rabbi Goldstein. "Do you have your tallit and tephillin?" he asked me.

"Yes," I replied.

"Okay," the rabbi said. "You have what you need. You can go on retreat now." And this from an Auschwitz survivor who lost his entire family!

One Yom Kippur, Rabbi Goldstein used the opportunity of the break in the daylong services to introduce congregants to a work called *Yosl Rakover Talks to God*. This work blew us away. Personally, I do not think I have ever read a more eloquent or moving piece about the Holocaust. Presumably, the piece was written by one of the last defenders of the Warsaw Ghetto. He writes his testament to God before immolating himself. He has a lot to say.

In his testament, Yosl Rakover recounts how he lost everything to wind up in the Warsaw Ghetto. A devout Hasid, he loses his work, his family, and his possessions but not his faith. Oh, his faith is obviously changed dramatically. No longer is he, in his words, a "Blind Amen sayer."[40] He describes himself as "bent but not broken."[41] He admonishes God for his actions with his children, the Jewish people. He questions God, as Job did. But he never loses faith. Neither did Job. Neither did *JB*.

Unlike Job of old, Rakover never gets his life restored to him. He must immolate himself rather than be captured by the Nazis. He is more like the heroes of Masada than the devout Job. But Job is a fictional story, a piece of literature. Masada was an actual event in which the defenders of the mountain fortress committed mass suicide rather than be taken captive by the Roman Army. Rakover takes the Masadan way out.

"How odd of God to choose the Jews," said anonymous graffiti. "It is not odd, the Jews chose God." The graffiti answered its own question (as the story goes). Rakover chooses God and keeps his faith. The Masadan defenders chose God and kept their faith. Job kept his faith, and all was returned to him. Nothing was returned to Rakover or to the last defenders of Masada (with the exception of the fact that members of the Israeli Defense Forces take their oath that "Masada will never fall again"). They are remembered gloriously, as are the three hundred Spartans at Thermopylae. The Masadan defenders left only a few people alive to tell the story. They wanted to be remembered.

Isn't it interesting that we can claim as heroes those who committed suicide. That is also how powerful Rakover's tale is. That is how powerful the story of Masada is. Glory is in self-sacrifice for a cause. In the case of the Jewish people, it was not just the cause of religion. It was the cause of *national self-determination*. These are the same causes that motivated the Maccabees and the Israeli defenders in 1948. Am Yisrael Chai! (The people of Israel live!)

It was some years later that I came upon the book *Yosl Rakover Talks to God* and learned that this piece was not real but rather the creation by one Zvi Kolitz from Argentina. I believe that Rabbi Goldstein might have thought that Rakover was a real person and that his testament was a real testament. I certainly never asked him or told him otherwise. I do not really know to this day if he revised his thoughts on this matter in light of Zvi Kolitz's book. Ultimately, it may not matter. Reading Yosl

Rakover was the first time I saw my oldest son (an infantry soldier) cry at a piece of literature. It is that powerful. But Rabbi Goldstein's survival was a matter of chance probability. That was true for everyone who survived. Yet he kept faith.[42]

Theodicy may be the most important question to be addressed by theo-philosophy. It is not a new question. It is the theme of *JB* cited before:

> If god is god, he is not good. If god is good, he is not
> god. Take the even take the odd. I would not sleep here
> if I could, except for the little green leaves in the wood,
> and the wind on the water.[43]

Was that the original Job's motivation? Was that Yosl Rakover's motivation? Was that Rabbi Goldstein's motivation?

There are many survivors. Some become atheists. Some abandoned any faith. Some got stronger in their faith. Some did not try to rationalize their survival. Some lost faith in human kind. Some got more faith in humankind. Some believed that they survived because it was God's will. Others felt they survived by chance. For the very devout, the Holocaust was the result of God's punishment for the sins of the Jewish people.

But what kind of deity would send one and a half million children into the sadistic hands of Josef Mengele and to the gas chambers, or to be tortured and buried alive, sometimes with their mothers and sometimes alone? And if such a deity does exist, is that the deity we want to worship? Yosl Rakover takes on the theodicy question eloquently—and given the topic, that is not easy.

From the time Rabbi Goldstein introduced us to the piece, *Yosl Rakover*, the theodicy issue became for me the most important theological issue to deal with in my life. Yes, I had been concerned about it before, as can be evidenced from *JB* and *Catch-22* being two of my most significant books. *Yosl Rakover* solidified the theodicy question as a central part of my theological and philosophical quests.

Being committed to core beliefs is not something trivial. Maintaining core beliefs in the face of clearly alternative evidence is a phenomenon that can be described in part as cognitive dissonance. Belief, disbelief, certainty, and uncertainty need to be studied and understood if we are to come to grips with truth at all. And human motivations in the face of adversities are complex phenomena. That is why *Yosl Rakover* has occupied a revered spot in my library since the day that Rabbi Goldstein introduced our congregation to it on Yom Kippur.

If you have been religiously indoctrinated since childhood, the theodicy question will create cognitive dissonance. Imagine the dissonance that a Holocaust survivor might feel if they had a traditional Jewish religious training and wound up at Auschwitz or Birkenau or Dachau or Treblinka or any other concentration camp of the Third Reich. Could you maintain a pure faith in God? Could you rest with the idea that we cannot understand God's ways and that this is ultimately all for the good?

The Holocaust was the logical result of almost two thousand years of Christian anti-Semitism in Europe, beginning in Rome when Constantine declared Christianity the national faith of the Roman Empire in the fourth century CE. I did not include *Constantine's Sword* in my list of determinative books because *Yosl Rakover* is the segue into anything related to theodicy. If you had to choose books, as I did for this project, making these distinctions of importance is real and sometimes even painful. James Carroll's tome *Constantine's Sword* is one of the most detailed and well-documented analyses of the catastrophe of the Holocaust that lays the ultimate evolution of the events at the feet of the Roman Catholic Church and European Christianity. It is critical reading for anyone interested in understanding the Holocaust and European Christianity. But you also must have access to the *Oxford English Dictionary* to read the work. It is erudite, factual, complete, and well documented. It is not without its own prejudices, as James Carroll is a Catholic priest who left the priesthood. On a side note, but of importance, is his book *Practicing Catholic*, which answers the question as to why he remained a Catholic in light of his research and ideas as expressed in *Constantine's Sword.*

Carroll lays out in extreme detail how the newly formed Catholic

Church villainized the Jews and how that villainization continued throughout centuries. Yosl Rakover presumably knew this history. Most educated Jews do. And yet he kept his faith.

Various modern scholars could, and sometimes do, take the position that the Holocaust also grew out of Germany's post-WWI despair and world economic collapse. Jews had been the traditional scapegoats in Europe for everything from the black plague to bad economies. But the true antecedents of the Holocaust in European Christianity are delineated in *Constantine's Sword* by James Carroll and rest clearly on the shoulders of Christian Europe.

Jewish anti-Semitism in Europe is a full investigation in and of itself. The role of the Catholic Church is likewise. So is the role of Martin Luther and his tirades against Jews (see *The Jews and Their Lies* by Martin Luther). The role of the Muslims is an additional but interwoven issue. Leave it to say that over almost two millennia, Europe was not a particularly safe place for Jewish people. This is why Theodor Herzl came to the conclusion that the Jewish people needed their own homeland in the state of Israel.

Theodicy is a central concern for people of faith as they try to understand something like the Holocaust. But there is another very serious question that may have a little less to do with God. The question is how can good people do bad things? How could intellectual German citizens turn into wanton and vicious killers and still go home to pat the dog and kiss their kids? How could physicians stand on the ramps and make selections and then return to their communities as practicing doctors? Some scholars feel that the question cannot be answered. Yet authors such as James Carroll, Noah Joshua Goldhagen, and Robert Jay Lifton, MD, seem to feel that they have a sense of an answer.

Let me deal with Christianity: Carroll and Goldhagen lay the Holocaust at the feet of Christian Europe, and particularly Christian Germany, with a long prodromal period beginning in the fourth century. Anti-Semitism had been woven into the fabric of the psyche of the European, and particularly part of the culture of being German, prior to WWII.

To be frank, anti-Semitism was so interwoven into German culture that the propagandists of the Third Reich had a fertile field to plow with their anti-Semitic agenda. Those agendas, throughout the medieval period and up to the Holocaust, harbored the thoughts of racial extermination to such a degree that when the killing became the solution to the "Jewish problem" in Europe, average German citizens were ready and willing to take on the task or look the other way. It should be noted that the Einsatzgruppen, the "police force" that followed Nazi troops into Eastern Europe and who had the express purpose of exterminating Jews (usually by shooting them at close range and burying them naked in mass graves), were often volunteers.

Goldhagen's book, *Hitler's Willing Executioners* (his doctoral dissertation at Harvard), is a chilling and detailed analysis of an answer to how good people could do horrific things. Carroll offers a similar and well-documented analysis in his book *Constantine's Sword*. Both date the anti-Semitism that led up to the Holocaust to the Catholic Church and later the Lutheran Reformation process. These "loving" Christian movements villainized the Jews and made determinations that would set the stage for the destruction of the Jews in Europe.

All the signs were therein Europe early on. The attacks on the Jewish communities of Worms and Speers in Germany on the way to the Crusades against the Muslims in Palestine, the pogroms, the ghettoization of the Jews, the massacres in Poland ... all foretold the Final Solution. Theodor Herzl determined that the Jew could not survive in Europe and so began the Zionist movement. No matter how assimilated they became, European Christianity would never let them succeed.

Robert Jay Lifton, in his book *The Nazi Doctors*, offers an additional solution. He documents the role of physicians in the Final Solution, beginning with the euthanasia killing of the disabled, the mentally ill, homosexuals, and Jews in the T4 program. Combining medical complicity with a program aimed first at those determined to have a "life not worthy of living" combined with the social engineering program of selective breeding to develop the master race, German physicians participated, if not led the way, to the Final Solution of the total annihilation of the Jews ("exterminationist anti-Semitism," according to Goldhagen). This effort would cleanse the German people of the "disease" and "infection" by the Jewish people.

Anti-Semitism is not limited to Christians. Many Muslims have it too, dating back to the seventh century when Mohammed was rejected by the Jews and they fought against him at Medina. They lost. Depending on which source one uses, there is one story that Muhammud, the Prophet and warrior for Islam, may have beheaded 700 Jewish soldiers who fought against him in Medina.[44] Muslim anti-Jewish anti-Semitism goes back to the beginning of Islam. So if there are approximately 2.7 billion Christians on earth and 1.5 billion Muslims,[45] that is a large universe of potential people who could be motivated against the Jewish people. It never made me feel awfully safe. Thankfully, I (would like to) believe that many, if not most, people today are not anti-Semites.

The problem between Muslims and Jews is at least as equally complex as between Christians and Jews. Islam is a daughter religion to Judaism, which in many ways is closer to Judaism than is Christianity. Islam has not just felt resentment at Jews not accepting Mohammed, as Christians have about Jews not accepting Jesus as Messiah and godhead. Both religions harbor feelings that if the Jews and their religion are not invalidated, then the daughter religions may not be true. It is only a matter of semantic debate as to whether these impulses are patricidal, matricidal, or fratricidal toward the original religion (Judaism).

For Germans, the issue morphed over time into a sense that Jews were irredeemable and were corrupt in and of themselves. Jews were the "disease" that was "infecting" the corporate body of the German people. For Muslims, on the other hand, there were periods of time in which Jews and Muslims (particularly Arabs) lived together in harmony. An example of this was Andalusian Spain. It was not until fundamentalist Islam reared its head in Spain that the Jews became at risk in al Andalus. Today, the Charter of Hamas expresses exterminationist anti-Semitism sentiments. Perhaps these issues were foundations as to why Arabs and Nazis got along together in common cause in WWII against the Jews.

These are areas for intensive study. The Film *Paper Clips*[46] reveals that this type of confrontation of the Holocaust can and does take place in America, on however complete or limited basis it may occur. Holocaust education in schools can give one hope.

These days, we read reports in the media that in Poland, it is now illegal to say that the Polish nation collaborated with the Nazis. Anti-Semitic incidents in France have been dramatically on the rise. Once again, Jews are at risk in Europe, in France, in Great Britain, and in the Middle East. Anti-Semitism in the US rose substantially between 2016 and 2019.[47] Assimilated German Jews could not understand what was happening in Germany. I fear that assimilated Jews in the US do not get it either. Assimilation is a powerful narcotic.

Read *Yosl Rakover* and then talk to me about this issue from both the perspective of theodicy and the perspective of humanity's inhumanity to humanity.

In 2013, for our fortieth anniversary, our sons sent us to Israel for the first time in our lives. This was a phenomenal trip that we could never have afforded to take ourselves. We did not take a tour but rather took a car and drove around the state. We only had enough time to cover much of the north of Israel. The one time we did take a tour was to Masada, as we would have to drive through the West Bank to get there. That was not recommended by our State Department. Going to Beersheba and up through Ein Gedi was much too far of a drive for us.

This trip was even more important to us because I had been diagnosed with a malignant prostate cancer twelve days before the trip. I was operated on a couple of weeks after return, but we decided to go to Israel despite the urgency of removing the cancerous prostate because I might not have that opportunity to be in the homeland again.

Debbie and I had taken a two-year certificate course in Jewish studies through Hebrew College, and I, having earned a master of science in Jewish studies and part of a doctorate in that field at Spertus College in Chicago, had amazing ammunition with which to go to the homeland. We wanted to experience Israel as secular Israelis. We never went to shul. Israel was our shul. We knew when Shabbat came and when it went. We went to the Kotel (Western Retaining Wall of the Second Temple), of course. We visited friends and a former professor. We immersed ourselves in history. We went to Caesarea, Masada, and the Dead Sea.

God came into the picture mainly at the Kotel. Like so many, I had a list of people to put good wish prayers into the wall on little pieces of paper. But I could not pray to a God I did not believe in anymore. I did not any longer hold the concept of an interventive deity. I thought long and hard about what to do at the Kotel. I arrived at a formula to say, "It should come to pass that so and so and so and so should have good health ..." This was a prayer I could say in good conscience.

Now, everyone has their own particular experience at the Kotel. We separated to go to the male and female sides of the Kotel. Debbie, as she related it to me, prayed there for me and for my recovery. I prayed for many but not for myself. When we got back together, Debbie asked where I was. She had looked over the mechitzah and was unable to locate me at the wall. "I was there under my tallit," I told her. "You couldn't have missed me." But she did not see me, and perhaps I was invisible ... merged with the Kotel and with all of Jewish history.

I wore my tallit gadol at the Kotel. Deb had bought it for me for my sixtieth birthday as my "big-boy tallit." Unfortunately, I did not bring my tephillin, which would have rounded out the experience.

After putting my written hopes and people's names on a slip of paper into a crevice in the wall, I then tried to pay attention to my own experience there. As I said, everyone has their own experience at the Kotel. I stood up against the wall and waited. Nothing happened. I covered myself in my tallit. Nothing occurred. "Okay," I told myself, "maybe I need to be in a meditative state." I pressed my entire body up close to the wall and put my tallit on the wall to form a tent for myself and began to listen to my breath. Finally, and abruptly, feeling the coolness of the wall and smelling its slight saltiness, I had a flood of imagery of the entire journey of our people. Scenes flooded my brain rapidly but not sequentially. The wall and I became one. Perhaps that is why Debbie could not see me.

Now, as the reader has guessed, I am not impressed by the mystical or metaphysical. But my experience at the Kotel told me that I was on the right journey. It was not about being closer to God. All I had to do for that was open my eyes, inhale the air, and appreciate being a conscious being in the universe. It was about being a Jew, with everything that means throughout history and the entire journey of the Jewish people. The Kotel is a part of that story but not its end.

I do not wish for the days of sacrificing animals to return. Yet the Kotel and the Temple Mount represent the ability of the Jewish people to have national self-determination. It is a political statement of national freedom as much as a religious one. And our people, the Jewish people, are alive and well in the State of Israel where we can live whatever Jewish life we wish in a land under our own self-determination. That is what the Maccabees fought for. It was what Bar Kochba fought for. And it was why the 1948 War of Independence was fought, why the Six-Day War was fought, and why the Yom Kippur War was fought. Am Yisrael Chai!

But what of religion? Yosl Rakover's faith in God as a noun might be tested in this book and set of concepts. An idea presented (*Everything Is God* by Jay Michaelson and *God Is a Verb* by Rabbi David Cooper) is that God is a verb and not a noun. That is to say that God does not intervene in the laws of physics on behalf of people, but rather, things happen as they must and not as they should because what we really mean by *god* is a verb. God is the entire process of the universe. How awesome is that concept! But this is also quite Kabbalistic, pantheistic, and probably panentheistic.

One of my rabbis once said to me that he felt that this stance was a lot of work to keep God in the picture. The whole process could make you out to be an *apikoros* (heretic).What I call the "unity principle" so central to Judaism is that whatever it (God) is, there is only one of it. Trinitarianism does not work for Jews any more than polytheism does. Monotheism is the hallmark of Judaism, as expressed in the watchword of Israel, "Hear O Israel, the Lord our G-d, the Lord is One."

Some translate *One* as "unique," and some translate it as "alone." Even Jewish atheists would tell you that if there is a god at all, then there is only one of it. What I call the unity principle reminds us that the entire universe is related to every part of that universe. It is all one thing. Everything is connected. If God is everything, and everything is the sum total of the universe, then the sum total is a unity. Many people have given up their lives to defend this monotheistic position.

Everything happens as it must—not as it should[48]or as we wish it to be. Can you pray to a verb? Not really. You can meditate. You can reflect to yourself. But what is lost with the idea of god as a verb and not a noun is the idealized image of a paternalistic entity who is interested in the affairs of men and women and is willing to intervene. Praying to God to intervene on our behalf is a hard mind-set to break.

There is a more practical side to these musings about religion. Let me discuss the evolution of my family's experience in America as illustrative.

I am only two generations removed from pogroms in Europe. My maternal grandmother (Nana, Ida Ostroff Levin) lived in Kovno Geburnia in Lithuania. She was silent about events there until much later in her life. But there were hints that something was very amiss in Europe during her childhood there before WWI. I did know that in World War II, within one month of the Nazi invasion of Lithuania, the Einsatzgruppen had murdered every Jew in Kovno Geburnia. I was made aware that the gentile citizens of Kovno used the Jewish gravestones in the Jewish cemetery as pavers for the roads thereafter. But I did not really know what happened when my grandmother lived there. Later in her life, she told me.

My grandmother was born on Christmas Day. Christmas was a day of pogroms in Eastern Europe. She refused to celebrate her birthday on December 25. Instead, she insisted that we celebrate it on the third night of Hanukkah. I did not really understand this until later in life when she began to speak of pogroms and of her remembrances of screams and rapes and murders and fires in her village. My great-grandmother (Ostroff) hid my grandmother under blankets in their house so that she would not be found by the marauding Christians.

A quick note of diversion: when the Ostroffsky (original name) family came in to Ellis Island (c. 1905), my great-uncle, who was only six at the time, was denied entrance due to the eye disease of trachoma. My great-grandparents had five other children. They sent my great-uncle back to Holland with another family who was not admitted to the US. He was never heard of again. My great-grandmother suffered major depression after that and was hospitalized at Metropolitan State Hospital in Boston. When we visited Ellis Island, I stood in the medical detention room where my great-uncle would have been denied entry into the US and that sealed his fate.

My paternal step-grandmother's first husband and two children were murdered in a pogrom in Russia. She had what we now diagnostically know as posttraumatic stress disorder (PTSD). She always had packed bags in case she had to escape quickly. Fresh water was in the refrigerator for the same reason. My father told me that if an unknown person knocked on the door, my grandmother might hide in a closet.

My parents were a transitional generation. They were born in the US in the twentieth century, unlike all of my grandparents who were born in Eastern Europe in the nineteenth century. When my grandparents were born, there was a czar on the throne of the Russian Empire. My grandparents felt that they were lucky to come to the US when they did. It meant that they and their descendants could live. They could be Jewish and survive. Had they not immigrated when they did in the early twentieth century before WWI, I would not be here to write this book.

While my grandparents spoke Yiddish at home and Yinglish (a fractured form of English mixed with Yiddish) outside the home, my parents only spoke the Mamaloshen (mother tongue) at home. In the outside world, they spoke English. They went to public schools, even though most of their friendship patterns and family patterns were Jewish. The State of Israel had not yet been founded when my parents grew up.

Growing up, my parents were becoming Americans with one foot in the shtetl Jewish community of Dorchester, Massachusetts. That neighborhood had all of the necessities of Jewish living: delis, kosher butchers, shuls, and so on. They attended public schools. They struggled to make a living. My father worked with my grandfather in his antique business. They married in 1939. Upon returning from WWII, they lived with my mother's parents in Dorchester. We moved to an apartment in Jamaica Plain when my father began to make enough money to have our own apartment. My father used the GI Bill to buy a house in the suburb of Newton. The Jews were leaving Dorchester in the 1950s to populate the suburbs of Brookline, Newton, Canton, and Sharon. They were becoming economically middle class.

Extended family also began to disintegrate. Uncle Hy Forman, who was terribly wounded in WWII, decided that he had to leave the cold of New England. He moved to Los Angeles and warmer weather. This was traumatic for the family. It was bad enough that the extended family was not together during WWII, but this would be the end of the shtetl style of living. Everyone knew that. Uncle Morry moved to Randolph, Massachusetts. It was near enough but not around the corner.

To maneuver the American world of the early twentieth century, one still had to be on the alert for anti-Semitism. My parents' generation would indeed assimilate and become economically successful, but the gentile world they were brought up in was still anti-Semitic. My parents' generation built grand synagogues (testimony to their success). They also built Jewish hospitals and nursing homes and schools. That was because Jewish doctors had a hard time becoming credentialed in gentile institutions, and colleges had quotas for Jews. Back then, occasional sign on hotels in some rural areas still announced, "No Dogs or Jews Allowed". This was when the film *Gentleman's Agreement* was made, representing institutional anti-Semitism.

To assimilate, many people changed their Jewish-sounding last names. In later years (especially for my generation), some people had cosmetic nose surgery to change their Jewish facial looks. They became what is known as twice-a-year Jews who were seen in shul only on Rosh Hashanah and Yom Kippur. When the State of Israel was founded in 1948, this brought forth a ground swell of Jewish pride. Every home had a Jewish National Fund (JNF) blue and white charity box in the kitchen. Our parents wanted my generation to be educated in Hebrew school and to have grand bar and bat mitzvahs. But they also wanted us to be part and parcel of the American experience.

I, on the other hand, grew up in Newton, Massachusetts. I went to public schools that were multiethnic but still predominantly Jewish. We experienced little anti-Semitism. Our world was still filled with delis, kosher butchers, and synagogues. It was easy to be Jewish. My world was filed with Jewish kids. It was part of the rhythm of life to go to public school, then Hebrew school, then come home to do English homework and then Hebrew homework.

With my family background, there was of course some degree of wariness about gentiles and their intentions. But our social intercourse with non-Jews was part of a great American success story for the Jewish people. Overt anti-Semitism was clearly reduced. We knew we had arrived when colleges let us in without quotas and when gentiles wanted to marry us.

Debbie and I made sure that when we had children, we moved to a Jewish neighborhood in Worcester, Massachusetts. We were walking distance to the shul and to the Jewish Community Center (JCC). Our kids went to the JCC for preschool, swimming, and Jewish activities. Two of them attended Solomon Schechter Day School (private Jewish school), and then all three of our children attended public school. They had Jewish camping experiences. But their world was not a shtetl. It was multiethnic. But they knew they were Jewish.

Today, our grandchildren are growing up in pluralistic communities. Our children did not specifically seek out Jewish communities in which to live and bring up children. You cannot be a rouge Jew. You cannot be Jewish as a rogue Jew. You need to have a community. It takes ten people for Jews to pray (a minyan). There is a reason for that. Jews are a communal people. Our god is not a personal god but a god of the nation. ("Kol Yisrael averim zeh l'zeh" or "All Israel is responsible, one for the other.") We are the Jewish people, not members of the Jewish religion.

No one can deny that anti-Semitism existed and still exists in America. In my lifetime, however, I have seen Supreme Court justices who are Jewish, a secretary of state who was Jewish, heads of major companies who are Jewish ... America has been a success story for the Jewish people. Success in America, for any ethnic group, can be a double-edged sword; on the one hand, you can become fully integrated into the dominant society, and on the other hand, you can lose your heritage. It takes no more than three generations for cultures to lose their original languages through assimilation. That is true for any culture, not just Jewish culture.

My grandparents suffered exterminationist anti-Semitism in Europe. My parents experienced a more prejudicial form of anti-Semitism in America. I barely felt anti-Semitism growing up. My children are rather removed from the issues of negative Jew/gentile relationships. I do not believe that my teenage grandchildren are concerned about this issue at all. My parents and my generation have been Jewish Americans. My children and grandchildren are American Jews and/or Americans with Jewish origins.

The extermination of the Jewish people was not a success of the Third Reich (even though they exterminated two-thirds of all European Jewry). It is becoming an accomplishment of American pluralism and assimilation. Especially for those Jews on the religious left, who believe that Judaism is a religion itself rather than the religion of the Jewish people (the Jewish nation), there will be a time in the near future when to be Jewish will not feel like a necessity. We will be fully assimilated. Christmas will be a secular holiday for many people of Jewish origin.

In the former Soviet Union, the Christmas tree was recast as the New Year's tree to keep the beloved Christmas tradition but to make it secular within a Communist atheist nation. It may be like that already in America for American Jews. It is that way for my grandchildren who, in one way or another, have Christmas as a secular holiday.

Given the history I have cited above, perhaps those who know me to have had some conflicts around Christmas may understand how and where those conflicts originated.

Jews even get cremated in America, just like gentiles. Auntie Rae wanted to be cremated. I told her, "Jews don't cremate."

"But everyone is doing it here in Florida," she retorted.

"Everyone is jumping off the Empire State Building," I said sarcastically.

"Don't be a funddy duddy," she said in retort.

"Six million ashes were not enough for you in this century?" I said.

"You win," my aunt conceded.

And she was buried as a Jew.

The caution here is that Jews are also now, and always have been, the canaries in the mine, the harbingers of social unraveling. Anti-Semitism is growing worldwide at an alarming rate. Once again, it is difficult to be Jewish on an American college campus. I have a great fear for the future. Could another Holocaust happen? If it does, as happened in Germany, even if you have a single grandparent who was Jewish, you would be eligible for the gas chambers. And the assimilated people had no idea why.

I continue to try my best for the continuity of the Jewish people. Even though my wife converted to Orthodox Judaism, I still have married into a family of Polish Roman Catholics and Greek Orthodox. Even though we tried to expose our children to holidays like Succoth and our grandchildren to Passover, it seems feeble to resist the powerful drug of assimilation. This is the common Jewish American story. Jewish intermarriage is greater than 50 percent. My family is no different.

I feel a tremendous sense of loss. I can look behind me and see the eradicated communities of Eastern European Jewry. I can look ahead of me and see a Judenrein America. Israel is our last, best hope for the survival of our people. We are not a religion like other religions. We are the Jewish people. We are the nation of Israel. Christianity has not superseded us. We are the people who chose justice as fairness over arbitrariness, who are fanatical about the care of the poor and needy, who gave the world such great additions to art, music, science, law, and medicine. We are a unique people who have survived despite everything and everyone who has tried to destroy us over millennia.

I feel like I am standing in the middle of an hourglass. The sands of the times of the past are running ever more quickly down into the glass that holds the sands of the times of the future. And soon I will be gone, and two generations later, no one will remember that I was here. They may not even know that I wrote this book for them.

My feeling is like the messenger in Job and of the allusion of Melville's character Ishmael in *Moby Dick*, "And I only am escaped alone to tell thee." And who will the good ship *Rachel*, Rachel who wept for her lost children, find as remnants of the Jewish people in the sea of the America of the future?

Such thoughts swarmed around my head during this time in my life. The 1980s–90s were cluttered up with all kinds of life events (that is how life is for so many at this stage of life). We became busy with children, Little League, skiing in the winter at our time-share in the Berkshires, camping, fishing, attending a Talmud study group every Monday evenings, bar mitzvahs, changes in work and geography, family illnesses, and so forth. Today, I feel an even greater sense of the urgency caused by confrontation of mortality.

I do, after everything, have a takeaway for *Yosl Rakover*. It includes the quote from a very old Pogo cartoon: "We have met the enemy, and he is us."

What *Yosl Rakover* tells us is *to stand by our Jewish posts* even in the face of industrial-level genocide and unspeakable evil. Perhaps that is the role of the Jewish people ... *to call out human evil* when it rears its ugly head.

"Shema Yisrael, Adonai, Elokhenu, Adonai Ehad." (Hear, O Israel, the Lord our God, the Lord is One).

Book 11

Words That Hurt, Words That Heal
by Joseph Telushkin, 1997

Do not spread (false) rumors among your countrymen.
—Leviticus 19:16[49]

Whoever shames his neighbor in public, it is as if he shed blood.
—BT, Bava Metzia 58b.

While *Yosl Rakover* presents existential issues, *Words That Hurt, Words That Heal* presents immanent issues ... matters of ethics and how we should be in the world. Ethics have always been extremely important to me. Since I was a little boy, I was concerned with people doing the right thing. Perhaps this was a part of my obsessive disorder. Perhaps it was emulating my father, who also had great ethical concerns (I think he had OCD also). Perhaps it was part of being Jewish. And since I teach college ethics, moral behavior has and is a great focus of attention for me.

To be a Jew is to be concerned with ethics, justice, and improving the world. Pirke Avot is an entire tractate of the Mishnah devoted to ethics. These three issues almost define what a Jew is. The entire tradition and life rituals are centered around continuous reminders of the facts that we should lead an ethical life, render justice as fairness, and do "deeds of loving kindness" that will lift up the world. This is the mission of the Jewish people, which they accepted upon themselves whether in partnership with God or on their own; to be an ethical people, and as such, a Light to the Nations. In the words of Proverbs 31:9, "Speak up, judge righteously, champion the cause of the needy and the poor."[50] This is the definition of a Jew!

A Jew's life is set up with many reminders to raise up the world and to be mindful. There are blessings for everything that is mundane and ordinary to make those things elevated to a higher level. There are blessings for eating, for seeing beautiful sights, for seeing Torah scholars, for going to sleep and for arising from sleep, for washing our hands, and even for going to the bathroom. A religious Jew's home has a mezuzah on every doorpost (except the bathroom) to remind us of the "Divine Laws" and our obligations as Jews to be ethical and just and to build up the world.

If there are reminders for what we put into our mouths, then there should also be concern for what comes out of our mouths. The mouth can be a devastating instrument. Many of us do not mind what we say, and what we say must be measured so as not to create harm. Yet when we speak, we need to watch what we say and how we say it. I know that I have needed this caution during my lifetime.

I was introduced to *Words That Hurt, Words That Heal* by my rabbi in 1997 while I was working in New Bedford as CEO of the Greater New Bedford Community Health Center, Inc. (GNBCHC). It is a wonderful book about "lashon harah" or evil speech. Lashon harah is Hebrew often pertaining to gossip but just as applicable to lying, perjury, ad hominems, attacking the character of others in public, and all other forms of harmful speech.

Early in *Words That Hurt, Words That Heal*, Telushkin tells an illustrative story about a person who had publicly embarrassed another person. After some time, the offender went to the offended person to seek forgiveness. He was informed that he could be forgiven if he took a feather pillow outdoors, cut it, and shook it out. He did and returned to the party he offended to again ask for forgiveness. He was told that he would first have to pick up all of the feathers. Upon protesting that this would be impossible, as the wind had scattered them, he was told that his embarrassing words were like the feathers. They could never be retracted, nor the harm they did. And like the feathers blown by the wind, the words had gone everywhere.

Human beings are such that we all have said bad things about other people, we all have spread rumors, we all have been the purveyors of bad language that may have embarrassed others, and we all lie. It is, unfortunately, a human trait of which we cannot be proud and must be mindful of.

The first place kindness begins is at home. That means that watching your mouth with your immediate family is more critical than what you do in business or out in the world. Yet the stresses of family life do not make this easy. There are no perfect parents, and there are no perfect children. There are no perfect husbands and no perfect wives. That means that things can be said in the heat of emotion that one inevitably regrets later. It is also true that marriage, at its best, is hard work. Harsh words between couples leave awful scars, yet who has not said them?

Married couples argue. Parents have conflicts with children. Children have conflicts with their parents. Siblings can have conflicts. Friends can argue. No one escapes unscathed. Harsh speech can be part of this whole scene, but it is one that we really have to work hard at not doing. Unconditional love is an ideal to strive for. But conditionalism is often what rules the day in the heat of emotions. These are not nice facts, but they are truisms in my life and my experiences. Utopian family life is probably unattainable even with people who are the most meaningful to you in your life.

In the Jewish tradition, seeking forgiveness directly from those who you have offended is a mitzvah on Yom Kippur (the Day of Atonement). It is important to do this with our work associates, our friends, and our families. Seeking real forgiveness from your spouse and children takes effort and courage if it is to be done with sincerity. That is why many people avoid this and do not even attempt the effort. I am no different. I have already noted that I have many regrets in life. My mouth during times of stress or anger is one of my most serious regrets.

After forty-seven years of marriage, my wife and I have not yet reached the marital utopian ideal. We still have plenty of conflicts. We still argue. We still hurt each other with words. We are still working on doing better. We are better with our children as they and we have matured. We are much better with our grandchildren in terms of expressing unconditional positive regard. We try to be delicate but truthful with our friends and business associates. But one still has to keep working at it. Watching one's mouth is the unending journey of being human. Certainly, this journey of watching what comes out of one's mouth is my own unending story.

In terms of business, I really needed this book when running the Greater New Bedford Community Health Center. Much of what I was involved with was political and required some serious negotiating and human management skills. Being able to be circumspect in what I said was a critical skill I had to employ. Running a large organization requires a good deal of care and control of one's mouth. It requires self-control.

In 1988, I left Rutland Heights Hospital to accept a position as associate director of human services at Hubbard Regional Hospital. The job entailed managing an outpatient mental health group, ER services, developing in-patient services, and consultative services. I clinically supervised a staff of about fifteen people and provided psychotherapy to patients. The latter was not where I wished to go professionally. I wanted the administrative side of human services. I began a job search.

In September 1990, I was offered and accepted the job as CEO at the Greater New Bedford Community Health Center. I began my work there unpaid from October to January, due to the financial condition of the community health center. We had a small staff of thirty-five who serviced poor and low-income people with primary care health services under the auspices of the Federal Bureau of Primary Health Care. The organization operated like a mom-and-pop shop since its founding in 1981. It saw about five thousand patients with 2.5 physicians in a nine-thousand-square-foot rented space with a $1.5 million budget.

By the time I left in 2007, I had built a 25,000-square-foot main health center and two secondary sites. I had acquired adjacent properties downtown in New Bedford, added services, including a full pediatrics program, geriatric services, lab, x-ray, dentistry, had a staff of some 250 persons with an $11 million operating budget ($14million gross, including free care), and helped bring about fluoridation of the water supply and cleanup of the city's brownfields. (See appendix B.)

None of this happened easily. All of it required political, negotiating, and organizational skills. Keeping it civil and managing conflict was a central part of my job. It really helped to be a psychologist, but it also helped to learn how to handle conflict and people's bad mouths, rumors, and backbiting. The environment was charged between the medical community and the community health center. This required a lot of personal control and savior faire on my part. It was stressful.

I organized one of the first mergers between a community health center and a health system (Southcoast) in the US, for which we won the Blue Ribbon Award for Innovation from the New England Healthcare Assembly. The merger helped us to get the revenue to expand our services, but it was not absolutely supported at the federal levels. They felt that the board would not be able to exercise its community governance control as a part of a larger system. We had already become a federally qualified health center (FQHC), a 340B Pharmacy site, and received accreditation by the Joint Commission on Accreditation of Healthcare Organizations (JCAHO). The merger occurred but required negotiation.

In such an environment, one really wants to be known as Ken Hartnett's article portrays me in appendix B. He was correct. I did not engage in disparaging of anyone during this process—no ad hominems, no blaming in public, and no obvious politics other than keeping people focused on the morality of providing care to the poor and needy of the community. In a city with some 57 percent of the population at or below two hundred percent of the poverty level, the strategy of keeping it on the civil up-and-up paid huge benefits. Not all organizations or leaders operated that way. But I did, consistent with what I had learned by experience and the books aforementioned. *Words That Hurt, Words That Heal* always reminded me to watch my mouth.

In front of the Greater New Bedford
Community Health Center, 2001

I am very proud of what I accomplished over the seventeen years I served the people of the Southcoast Massachusetts region. Tens of thousands of people got healthcare because of my efforts, as my board president once reminded me. I am really proud of Ken Hartnett's article, and I read it every time I feel that my ego needs boosting (see appendix B). This is how I wanted to be remembered ... as a good man with a good reputation, doing good for people. You can achieve that if you stay close to morality, stay objectively oriented, and watch your mouth.

This is not to give the reader the impression that my mouth was guarded in a saintly way. I made plenty of verbal mistakes. I could be accused of using foul language. Sometimes I could make mistakes that were hurtful to people. But from a political point of view, I managed my mouth fairly well.

I will say that over time, I have learned that in the heat of adrenaline or when coming out of anesthesia (without full inhibitory cortex control), I can be a bear. I am not proud of that. But it can be the case.

Beyond my professional life, there were plenty of psychosocial stressors during this period. My oldest son left for the army in 1995. That year, we moved from Worcester to the New Bedford area to reduce my four hours on the road every day (I stayed over in New Bedford when I had night meetings, etc.).My mother took ill, and we moved her in with us. My two younger sons changed schools from Worcester to Dartmouth, we went from a Conservative shul to an Orthodox shul (much to my family's chagrin), and I had to professionally keep things afloat organizationally, strategically, and financially for a growing community health center.

Stress was the key word for this season of my life. It all took a great toll on me, my wife, and on my family. I lasted seventeen years as CEO of the Greater New Bedford Community Health Center. Some of my colleagues succumbed to the stress. I worried I might be like that too. It was a challenge to lead an organization that had a primary mission to poor and disenfranchised people. It took all of the organizational, conflict-management, and social skills I had. It also did not hurt that I was a psychologist.

In terms of *Words That Hurt, Words That Heal,* I must say that I have said evil speech more than one time. I have a temper and can say bad and hurtful things. I often use the "F" word thanks to years of treating alcoholics and combat Vietnam veterans. I can be cruel. I have found that when coming out of anesthesia, I can be especially ill-tempered and short with people. It has been said of me that, like my father, I do not suffer fools lightly. I can be sarcastic. I can be critical. "For all O God of forgiveness, forgive us, pardon us, atone for us" (to quote the confessional liturgy of Yom Kippur).[51]

No one escapes their own mouths. It is a full-time occupation to be kind and compassionate, long on patience, and pleasant of speech. At least it is for me.

Fear and anger are terrible things. Fear leads to anger, and anger can lead to rage. In animals that cannot talk, they can become assaultive and bite when threatened. You can see this in dogs. Even though domesticated, when afraid or enraged, they can express themselves by biting. Young children who have not yet acquired language may do the same. Adults do it with words—words that can create suffering. I have lost friends over bad words.

Two incidents I remember include a close friend who showed his true colors one night when he was intoxicated at a party. In a discussion about manliness, he blurted out to me, "A Jewish man is not a man." I got up and left immediately. Our relationship was unsalvageable thereafter.

I do have to say that despite my Jewish commitment from childhood on, I really did not experience rampant anti-Semitism. I knew about it, but my personal experience of it was low. I never felt that my Christian friends could harbor anti-Semitic feelings. So, when this event happened, it woke me up to how insidious anti-Semitism could be. I was impressed by how a Christian person could harbor such thoughts without expressing them until alcohol loosened the lips. "In vino veritas" as the expression goes. And this truth was not pleasant to confront.

The second incident overtly concerned politics and the sharp divisions in the US in the Trump era. As you have seen throughout this manuscript, my tendencies are toward the liberal side of politics. One close friend had developed himself to be on the right. At one point, he told me that my politics meant that I had allied myself with those who "despise" America. Now one should never say that to anyone of good conscience but certainly not to one who has an honorable discharge from military service and carries a copy of the US Constitution with him to work. That was the end of our longtime friendship. Words matter.

Earlier, I described morality as *the decrease of suffering and increase of well-being*. When we use bad speech, we are not moral by this definition. In fact, we are just the opposite.

What I have discovered through writing this book and examining the speech we use seems to be reinforcement of the determinism of the unconscious mind. When dark things lurk in the unconscious (as they do for us all), then under certain conditions, those things can come out. Because we are speaking primates, we can express those dark, unconscious things in language. Controlling the mouth is so difficult and requires such conscious attention.

When it does come out, it can shock us. It can run deeply against the self-image we create for ourselves about ourselves. No one likes to see themselves as evil. But both righteousness and evil exist within each of us. There is no pure person.

But that does not mean that if we are consciously committed to improving the world, we should not work on controlling our mouths. Hurting others verbally, in the Jewish tradition of the Talmud, is equated to murdering a person. "He stands in Syria and kills in Rome"[52] goes the expression about lashon harah.

Now all of this has implications to the Holocaust as well. Goldhagen, in his opus magnum, *Hitler's Willing Executioners*, explores the complicity of the German and other occupied European peoples who brought the Jews to the gas chambers and killing fields, both actively and passively. Hitler could not accomplish the Final Solution by himself. He needed an entire nation to do that. Anger, motivated by fear, is a powerful tonic. It can strip away our civilized selves to expose the violent apes that we are. We do not have canine teeth for nothing. Propaganda in the service of prejudice is the penultimate example of lashon harah.

Propaganda in the Third Reich was a high art form. But it was built on conspiracy theories like years of "blood libel" stories that Jews kidnapped Christian babies to use their blood to bake matzot on Passover, or the likes of *The Protocols of the Elders of Zion* published in Russia, which purported that there was an international cabal of Jews bent on world domination through control of financial markets.

Evil speech is the beginning of prejudice. And prejudice is the beginning of apartheid, and apartheid is a segue to genocide. Lurking within us are dark forces indeed. Those can be projected out onto scapegoats for our self-loathing. I am convinced, somewhat based on the work of Temple Grandon (*Animals Make Us Human*), that bad words begin in fear, and fear begets anger, and anger begets rage, and rage begets lashon harah and all of its consequences. This may be a process common to all mammals but intensified in humans because we have the use of language.

The biblical story in the Torah of Azazel is not there for nothing. Sending Azazel (the scapegoat) into the wilderness after the high priest has confessed the sins of the nation on its head is a metaphor for the antecedents of prejudice, apartheid, and genocide, for which we must atone. Dark forces indeed need to be expunged.

Dark forces lurk within us, and unless we confront them, they can do severe damage. Even churchgoing people are not exempt. I am always mindful of the fact that the Holy Inquisition, which brought torture, maiming, and death to so many, was authorized by the pope—the holy father. Similarly, the American post-bellum lynchings of black, Mexican, and Native American people were often attended by crowds of "normal" Americans. As if hanging (of both sexes) and shootings were not enough for the expression of communal extrajudicial rage, victims could be publicly whipped, tortured, maimed, and burned alive. Sometimes this horror went on for hours to the delight of the crowds. People often attended these executions as if they were picnics, bringing their children to witness the horror while munching on sandwiches in their dress-up finery. When victims were mutilated, their body parts (such as fingers) might be sold or given away to crowd participants as souvenirs. This is a grim part of American history.

Then, of course, there were the Salem witch trials, the massacres of Native Americans, and so on. Germany was not the only nation afflicted by evil. Genocide and massacres have occurred all over the world, in Serbia and Croatia, in Cambodia, in Ruanda, in Yemen, in Syria, in ISIS-controlled territories, and the list goes on. Even in "civilized" France, there was a post-revolutionary reign of terror and many public beheadings.

And these processes often began with evil speech about people different from the general community. Extrajudicial killings occurred when people were accused by rumors, gossip, and falsehoods. Without the rule of law, the mob could take over, and not infrequently, such mobs consist of normal churchgoing individuals. These are the same people who express value for the concept of love of neighbor as a divine command. Hypocrisy is the handmaiden of rage and self-hatred. Evil speech is its harbinger.

A favorite propaganda tool has always been to link the target group with words like *infection, disease,* or *infestation.* During the black plague, this tactic was used against Jews in Europe. Goebbels used this tactic against Jews and gypsies during the Third Reich. The Trump administration uses this tactic against Mexican and Central American people. It is not only dehumanizing but creates fear in the majority population. It is lashon harah!

We have already cited Sartre's work on anti-Semitism. Eric Hoffer suggested that self-loathing might underlie evil mass movements in his works *The True Believer* and *The Ordeal of Change.* It is just amazing to me how much we humans do not like ourselves and how covered up by psychological overlay those feelings are.

These forces are, and have been, commonplace in the human experiment—even in the most democratic of countries. In 2020, in America, we have seen the power of words wielded from the very top levels of government—words that malign the free press, anyone who disagrees with administration policy, African people, Central American people, people of liberal political leanings, intellectuals. We have heard all this kind of language before out of the mouth of Dr. Joseph Goebbels, Pol Pot, and Chairman Mao. Words cannot only hurt. Words can kill.

Words That Hurt, Words That Heal is the segue book into this entire discussion. It has been good for me to reflect on this personally and as to what it means to our species. It would be good for everyone to read Telushkin's book.

I try to impress upon my philosophy students how powerful words are. Words create pictures of reality for us, as Ludwig Wittgenstein told us.[53] Words can be ambiguous. Words have the power to hurt or the power to relieve suffering. Words are our major form of communication.

But words need to be used carefully, and few of us are that consciously reflective most of the time. Using words carefully is a full-time occupation and requires us to be aware and alert.

There is a great Buddhist story about the Buddha being encountered by some people who saw that there was something different about him. They asked him, "Are you a god?"

"No," he answered.

"Are you an angel?" they inquired further.

"No," he answered.

"Are you a messenger?" they queried.

"No," he said.

"Well, if you are not a god, and you are not an angel, and you are not a messenger, what are you?"

"I am awake," he concluded.

To be awake should be a goal of life, especially when we are using words. This requires significant discipline, awareness, and the ability to apologize. Being awake is a full-time occupation.

Controlling our mouths is one of the most important things we can do in a life of mindfulness if we are really interested in reducing suffering and increasing well-being. What comes out of the mouth should be as important to living as what we put into the mouth. My mother used to tell me, "If you can't say something nice, don't say anything at all." I think that many mothers said that adage to their children.

Saying and doing are two different things. We always judge a person's real values through their behavior and not their words alone. That is the dilemma of lashon harah. You cannot just talk the talk. You have to walk the walk. I am afraid that in the scheme of things, this is a goal to strive toward rather than a destination at which to arrive. Being fully conscious takes a huge amount of mental energy, which most of us have difficulty with. I know that is true for me.

I wish I could take back all of the negative things I have verbalized throughout my life. Despite all of the negative things my father said to me, the one thing I missed him saying was "I love you." I know that he did (in his way), but had he verbalized it, that would have made the course of my life different. I know that I have probably said bad things to my kids as well. But I make sure to say "I love you" in words and, hopefully, in deeds. In fact, we are judged more by what we do than by what we say.

If the reader will indulge me a moment of free association. One of my sons reminded me recently of in incident when we were fishing in Canada. I took each of my sons to Forest City, New Brunswick, when they were ten, as my father had taken me in 1957. Well, one year, my oldest son took a big four-wheel red ATV and, despite protestations, ran it dangerously near an embankment. Of course, he and this few-hundred-pound machine toppled down a hill, with the machine landing on top of him.

No one ever saw me run so fast. I tripped over a branch on the ground, fell on my chest, bounced up, and kept running to the machine. I covered a distance of about fifty or more yards in seconds. With a huge amount of adrenaline pumping, I lifted the ATV off of my son. I think I weighed in at about 140 pounds at the time.

I saved my son from what could have been a tragedy. How I lifted the ATV, I still have no idea. But I did it. If that is not love, what is? I did not care about anything else except saving my son. All the "I love you's" in the world would take second place to my actions that day. My son still tells the story humorously. When I tell the story, I am still scared to death! Doing is more of a test than saying. We are judged by our actions, not our thoughts.

After a good amount of self-criticism above, I think that it may be important to discuss being on the receiving end of lashon harah. It is not pleasant. Lashon harah creates suffering and decreases the sense of well-being and safety. This can be especially true when people are nice to your face yet talk badly about you behind your back. I have been the victim of this kind of lashon harah many times. I think it can come with the territory of being both a leader and an intellectual. But I have also experienced it from supposed friends. It hurts.

I have an image of myself as a decent person. When I find out that some people interpret me differently and speak about me in forums where their negative thoughts and words can get back to me, it hurts. I would much prefer that people tell me what they think of me to my face. "The truth will make you free, but first it will make you miserable." I have had my share of feeling betrayed and miserable. These are the bitter blows of life and the joys and burdens of leadership. When you put yourself out there in a community, such things can happen to you. Well, even if you don't leave home, as we all have seen during our confinement for COVID-19, people can still talk badly about you.

Without the possibility of face-to-face confrontation, people seem to feel a less restricted sense of what they can or cannot say. Facebook is good example. The viciousness that occurs on that social medium is astounding. I really wonder if people would be so cruel, mean, and vicious if they had to be face-to-face with the person they are maligning. I could not take Facebook and deleted my account. People on that medium made me angry and sad.

Being in service to a community means you have to have skin like a duck or hide like a rhinoceros. But at the same time, even the toughest of people can be hurt by bad talk and ill will. Disappointment with those with whom you have felt a good relationship, only to be betrayed by finding out that they spoke against you in private, is ultimately disturbing.

I have also found that when you have success, others may reject you either out of jealousy or their own self-deprecation projected onto the successful person. This can be true when one has financial success, business success, or academic success. I have found that there are many people who dislike intellectuals. Even if you do not feel superior to others who do not have your education or opportunities, one must realize that there are those who will dislike you and reject you simply because you are an intellectual.

I am afraid that it does no one any real good to hide their intellectualism or business success. That is disingenuous as well. You do not have to flaunt success or intelligence, but hiding it does not help either. Still, no one wishes to be the brunt of others' ill will. So, there is a dilemma. Human beings really do not like others to get ahead.

It is always fascinating to me how people are interested in English royals but also go out of their way to find fault with them. People do this with movie stars and captains of industry as well. We are jealous of success but also wish to take down those who are succeeding. That process can and does lead to lashon harah. There is an entire industry of tabloid magazines that thrive off of this process.

Lashon harah is a viscous beast that plagues us all at an unconscious level. Overcoming both the saying of lashon harah and being on the receiving end are hard issues to deal with. Let's face it: human beings can be very nasty to one another. Being kind is a full-time occupation. But if the reduction of suffering and increase of well-being are goals worthy of human attainment, then we have a lot of hard work to do. I know this by having been both on the giving out and receiving end of lashon harah.

People are not naturally kind. Sometimes what looks like kindness is actually the sublimation of hostility. In both cases, we must be on guard, consciously aware, empathetic, and aware. I am not sure there is anything more important. "Love your fellow as yourself" are nice words but very inadequate to the human process. Chapter 3, Mishnah 2 of *Pirke Avot* tells us to "Pray for the welfare of the government, since but for the fear of it men would eat each other alive." Shimon, the son of the great Talmudic sage Gamliel the Elder, advises us in Chapter 1, Mishnah 17 in *Pirke Avot* that "I have found nothing better for a person than silence … and whoever speaks excessively causes sin." I love Jewish ethics and the wisdom of the great Jewish sages.

I should like to offer a reflection on lashon harah and political correctness. Many of us in my generation grew up with racism, sexism, ethnocentrism, and fear of those outside of our community. The role of *in* and *out* groups is a social phenomenon. While the efforts of social egalitarianism in the 1960s aimed at creating a more gentle and equal society, it failed. The forces of the in and out-group phenomena are very strong, very real, and very hard to overcome. That means that they are ingrained and unconscious phenomena that require our attention and awareness.

As a college teacher, I am very sensitive to these issues. On campus, people are quite concerned about language and micro-aggressions. Sometimes, I fear, this has gone overboard. But that does not diminish the history of offenses committed verbally against one or another group both on and off campus.

It is not wrong to be politically correct in our speech without being so politically correct that we find that we cannot say anything at all. When an offense is made, one certainly needs to apologize for it. It is, of course, even better to be aware enough so as not to offend at all. But this is not fully possible. All of us have a reservoir of ideas from our own families, ethnic and racial upbringings, and sex. This is one more area where I believe one must strive to be better without the oppression formed by the unattainable nature of the outcome. "Perfect" is crazy, and we should not expect that in ourselves or others.

That does not mean that we should accept unmitigated nastiness. We all need to work at watching our mouths, some more than others. In social intercourse with people who are different from us, the standard of the golden rule should reign. Treat others as you wish to be treated is a gold standard of intergroup relations. Or, even better is Hillel's version, "That which is detestable to you, do not do to others."

Human beings are like entities that are half-angels and half-animals. We have really big brains, but we also have canine teeth. What a dilemma for our species, for you and for me. Our evolution has left us in this dilemma. But that does not mean that we should not strive toward kindness, compassion, and empathy. It is in the striving that we can find our higher selves and bring peace between people and to the world. That may not make the hurt and harm from lashon harah any easier, but it might give us hope and understanding.

Even if free will is actually less influential than we thought, striving to control our speech is a laudable pursuit. And where we fail in that regard, apology can be curative. And in all cases, we need the rule of justice as fairness. In the inimitable words of the Talmudic sages of blessed memory, "Pray for the welfare of the ruling power, since but for the fear of it, men would swallow each other alive."[54]

So, here is my take away from Telushkin: ***Watch your mouth!***

Book 12

Who Wrote the Bible? by Richard Elliot Friedman, 2003

What are we to do with this knowledge?[55]

I have a great love of Judaism and for the Jewish people, as the reader must certainly understand by now. I have been a committed Jew my entire life. Sometimes, this was much to the chagrin of my family and some of my friends. I was a devout praying person and turned to God in times of distress. These times were frequent, and the answers to my prayers never came … or if they did, they could have been explained by random probability. They never salved my obsessive anxiety concerns or my mental pains.

On a psychosocial basis, I have always been devoted to the Jewish people, to their contributions to the human experiment, to their ethics, and to their mission of being a Ner L'Goyim or a Light unto the Nations. That is expressed not only in law and ethics but also in the fact that we have per capita the highest number of Nobel laureates of any ethnic group. Our contributions to the human experiment in science, medicine, law, finance, politics, the arts, and music are great. Who is better at comedy than Mel Brooks, or filmmaking than Steven Spielberg, or physics than Albert Einstein? And the list goes on.

My evolution in my own Judaism and in my life came through study, study, and more study, as well as personal suffering. Today, the people on the Jewish right would consider me an apikoros (heretic), however, because I subscribe to higher text criticism. The people on the left, not so much. But I do appreciate orthopraxis. My journey has been an arduous one and sometimes one in which two competing positions were maintained at the same time. That is a particularly Jewish position to be in; is this true or is that true? Yes!

There are two great tragedies in my life—the fact that I, like David Weiss Halivni, feel that "the people I daven" (pray) "with I cannot talk to and the people I talk to I cannot daven with"[56] and that I was less successful than I had hoped in definitively contributing to the continuity and well-being of the Jewish people on my watch. But I continue to live a Jewish life, to try to accommodate the polar opposite forces I have outlined above, and to study. That brings us to the Bible.

My first encounter with the Bible (Hebrew Scriptures) as literature was through one of my Talmud chaverim (friends or study partners) who was a professor of English and taught such a course. That was back in the 1980s. So, I must say that by the time I reached the Me'ah program (adult Jewish learning) at Hebrew College in 2003, I was already acquainted with the concepts of the documentary hypothesis and higher text criticism. These hypotheses considered the biblical text to be of human origin.

Debbie and I took the Me'ah certificate course at Hebrew College in 2003–5 through the Jewish Federation of Greater New Bedford, of which I served twice as president. The Me'ah program is a one-hundred-hour two-year program of Hebrew College aimed at adult Jewish education. Professors came from universities near and far to teach the various classes that began with the question *Who Wrote the Bible?* and the book of the same title. We were fortunate to have professors of renown from Brown University, Hebrew College, and as far away as Ben Gurion of the Negev University in Israel. Although we would read Friedman's book in 2003, I was familiar with the concepts that I learned in the 1980s in our Talmud group.

The period of the 1980s to the 1990s was an interesting period for me religiously, personally, and professionally.

During the late 1980s through the early 1990s, our sons became bar mitzvahs. We wanted to keep the focus of those events on the religious aspects and not the lavish party aspects. All of the members of our Talmud group learned to *lehn* (chant) Torah for the bar mitzvahs and were included thereby in the events. The kids did great jobs. But even with Jewish day school, Jewish summer camps, and Hebrew high school, the Benei Mitzvah[57] is normally the first day in a Jewish child's life when he is never seen in shul again (as the common Jewish parental wisdom goes). And so it was for our kids too.

This left me saddened, guilty, and alone ... but still on my own quest. "What did I do wrong?" has become the American Jewish parent's lament. Perhaps it is just living in a pluralistic society that is the issue. The matter is not uncommon in Jewish American family life. That is evidenced by so many shuls closing and/or merging.

Besides my Jewish angst, there were other secular events that occurred in the late 1980s that threw me into a mental depression and anxiety condition. One event brought me very much into the public eye in Massachusetts politics and public service. I received the Manual Carballo Award for Excellence in Public Service in 1987, given by Governor Michael S. Dukakis. Winning the award entailed an award dinner in front of a huge crowd of people at the Park Plaza Hotel in Boston, newspaper articles, $1000 cash (which was not insignificant in 1987), and your name being but on a bronze plaque in the governor's office at the State House. The award is the highest honor in public service in the commonwealth—very prestigious.

One of the achievements was my work founding the Bradford R. Burns PTSD Unit at the MA Department of Public Health Hospital, Rutland Heights Hospital. This was, at the time, the only public health hospital-based program for combat Vietnam veterans in the United States. That was very consistent with the commonwealth, which started the Office of the Commissioner of Veterans Services in 1864. Additional professional attention was also paid to this program because the acting commissioner of public health and I published a significant professional article on the project in *Public Health Reports*[58] as well as when Governor Dukakis ran for president.

In front of the Bradford R. Burns PTSD Unit
at Rutland Heights Hospital, 1987

Other professional accomplishments for which I received the Carballo Award included my work in addictions rehabilitation, adolescent addictions programs, the MA Second Offenders DUI project, and the development of a neurobehavioral unit at Tewksbury Hospital (MA Department of Public Health). I was also appointed to the faculty at the UMass Medical School as assistant professor of family and community medicine, teaching addictionology, trauma, and public health. My teaching colleague and I published our research on the teaching of addictions and presented at the Society of Teachers of Family Medicine[59] ... more attention.

Anyone who is familiar with the Rah scale of psychological stressors knows that winning awards can be as much stress as something negative. My stressors had been building over years. By 1986, everything began to come to a head. I began to become morbidly obsessive and anxious about my life as a psychologist in a private practice, the currency of my education, my public practice with the MDPH, my religious life, my children's lives, finances, and so on ... the entire catastrophe of life.

Public recognition only stimulated more anxieties for me. I felt that my nontraditional doctorate's currency was not good enough, that I really was not as smart as people were crediting me for, and so on. How could I win awards like this when I felt unworthy of such recognition? Most of this stemmed back into childhood and my inability to please my father. Things got so bad by 1987 that I sought psychiatric help, as I have noted. I pulled it together, but two decades later, in 2007, I found myself back in a psychiatrist's office, crushed by responsibilities, loss, physical disease, and the resulting symptoms of obsessiveness.

One of the features of an obsessive personality can be religiosity. It is one way to try to handle anxiety. It certainly was a way I used to handle my anxiety. Unfortunately, I never received the salve I needed from prayer and immersion in Jewish practice. Nothing took my anxieties away. Immersion in work was the best I could do to free myself. Fishing and hiking did not hurt either. Meditation helped. Psychiatry helped. But the harder I worked at my religious life, the less reduction of anxiety and suffering I received and the more alienated my children seemed to become from my form of practice of Judaism.

Despite all of this, I continued my Talmud studies passionately. Our Worcester Talmud Chavurah group met every Monday evening for two hours. Once we moved to New Bedford, I founded a Talmud study group in that community. I was never sure as to whether this intensive form of Talmud study helped or hurt my obsessiveness.

I had read Freud's *Moses and Monotheism* years before and understood the psychoanalytic concepts regarding religion and unconscious workings of the psychic apparatus. But the obviousness of the human origin of the texts did create some dissonance. As a Jew participating in the Conservative movement, the idea of divine inspiration was still a lively one for me to counter the dissonance of the text not having a divine origin at all. I lost that over time.

The fundamental hypothesis of higher text criticism and the documentary hypothesis are that the biblical texts are not of divine origin but of human development. Scholars have discovered four separate authors of the Torah. "E" is that text that most often uses the term

Elohim for God. It is a text presumed to have been written in the Northern Kingdom of Israel sometime in antiquity until 722 BCE. "J" is that text that most often uses the name YHVH or Jehovah for the name of God. It is presumed to be written in the Southern Kingdom of Judea sometime around c. 900–586 BCE. The "P" text is the text that concerns itself with ritual and jurisprudence. It is assumed to express the concerns of the Aaronide priesthood writing in late Judea and into the Babylonia Exilic period. "D" text includes Deuteronomy and is presumed to be the text discovered by Hilkah the priest and brought to King Josiah of the Southern Kingdom of Judea in the seventh century BCE. However, scholars also agree that D also represent the Deuteronomistic history, including the books of Joshua, Judges, Samuel 1 and 2, and Kings 1 and 2. There were also redactors of the E and J texts. That would account for eleven of the twenty-four books of the Jewish canon, the TANAK.

Other issues cast doubt on the text. Those include historical and archaeological findings. For example, there is no evidence to confirm the legend that 603,550 men at arms and their families, amounting to 2.5–3 million persons, camped in the Sinai Desert for forty years and left not one shred of archaeological evidence of their sojourn. Similarly, there is no evidence for a worldwide flood some five thousand years ago. And the historical and archaeological evidence against the authority of the text as an accurate historical record goes on.

Ultimately, one may intellectually conclude that the Bible is of human origin and represents the concerns and tensions of the late Bronze and early Iron Ages. It is a literature of rich legends and myths. But it also is foundational step forward in jurisprudence. The Torah cannot stand on its own without the Talmud. The tradition is that there is the written law (Torah) and the oral law (Talmud). Otherwise, the written Torah sounds just as arbitrary and capricious as other Bronze and Iron Age texts. It is the Talmud that brought us from the religion of biblical Israel to Rabbinic Judaism.

Then Steven Hawking published *A Brief History of Time*, and it became even clearer to me that God could be a mental construct. Even though Hawking finished his book with a reference to the "mind of god," I suspected that he was really an atheist, as so many physicists were. In his book *The Grand Design*, Hawking and Leonard Mlodinow are pretty clear about their feelings that God is not a necessary concept to hold in physics or for the creation of the universe. The big bang could have happened spontaneously with or without the intervention of a creator deity. So where would that leave me? Well, one did not have to throw away the concept of God, but one did have to redefine what that concept meant.

In later years, I became disheartened about my own Judaism. I did have a later career as a Jewish professional where I helped communities that had to merge their Jewish organizations due to changing demographics and so on. I became expert in that field. In 2009–10, I facilitated the merger of the Jewish Federation, Board of Jewish Education, and the Jewish Community Center to become the Jewish Alliance of Greater Rhode Island. In 2012, I did the merger of the Jewish Federation, Jewish Community Center, and Jewish Family Service to become the Jewish Community Alliance of Northeastern Pennsylvania. I served as the CEO for the Jewish Community Alliance of Northeastern Pennsylvania in 2016–17. I was twice president of the Jewish Federation of Greater New Bedford and once its treasurer. I had served as a member of a synagogue board of directors and as a member of its Hebrew School Committee. I served on the Advisory Committee for the Center for Jewish Culture at the University of Massachusetts, Dartmouth. I authored articles on Judaic issues in both Jewish and secular publications and wrote the introduction to the JFNA publication of mergers and acquisitions. I taught adult Jewish education at three synagogues and two chavurot. I hold a certificate and advanced degree in Jewish studies. I have had a significant Jewish set of life experiences.

I have come to realize that our texts are of human origin and that they reflect the tensions and concerns of far earlier ages. They are not, in my humble opinion, of divine origin (that statement alone makes me an apikoros to those on the right). They combine legend and jurisprudence as the Talmud combines *aggadah* (stories) and *halachah* (law) into a single text. Jewish literature and theology is *progressive*. In this respect, the Reform tenet of progressive revelation may be more correct. Whether there is such a thing as revelation rather than enlightenment, it is all still progressive ... perhaps even a Hegelian dialectic process. But we do still have a foundational document (Torah) and theology upon which rests our entire journey. It might be incorrect to discard the entire journey for the sake of modern enlightenment about the origins of that sacred document.

I would like to spend just a moment on the words *revelation, enlightenment, progressive,* and *evolutionary.* When I speak of revelation versus enlightenment, what I mean by those terms is that in enlightenment, one becomes aware by their own effort of something one did not know before. What I mean by revelation is that one becomes aware of something of hidden meaning through the agency of an external source. In terms of the words *progressive* versus *evolution,* I mean that progression is the process through which things develop from one thing to the next, usually in a more adaptive direction. Evolution, to me, implies that things move from one state to the next in some more random manner than proceeding toward any particular goal or state of being. So, when I state that the Reform are "more correct" about the issue of progressive revelation as a central tenet of that movement, I am saying the idea of forward motion in the development of thought is more consistent with modernity than is a static revelation in antiquity. But that is not to say that I agree with progressive revelation in either progression or in revelation. I agree more with the idea of enlightened thought through personal agency, which may or may not have any particular goal or truth revealed by an external agent.

I spend time on words because without a thorough understanding of what the sender of a message means, the receiver of the message may confuse the intent and description of the message itself. I am deeply devoted to understanding language and its use. As such, I value Ludwig Wittgenstein, whose focus was on the use of language, as one of the greatest philosophers of the modern era.

I relate all of this to underscore the evolution I have gone through both intellectually and religiously. It has been a long, slow process. It has not been easy. And, in my opinion, this evolution had a lot to do with my mental status as well. It has been a part and parcel of how I have dealt with anxiety.

After my bout with obsessive anxiety in 1987, I improved a lot. I improved enough to leave my job at Rutland Heights Hospital in 1988 (which I held since 1975) and pursue other things. A colleague of mine recruited me to become associate director of human services for the Hubbard Regional Hospital just south of Worcester. I accepted the job on the understanding that this would be an administrative job. It turned out to be a clinical one as well as administrative. That was not the direction I had planned to head in at that point.

I had already decided to leave clinical work in pursuit of my administrative interests. Thanks to Dr. Bruner, I had become a member of the American College of Healthcare Executives, and administration was the direction I felt that I had to go in. I was done with clinical work with alcoholics, drug abusers, and PTSD combat survivors. You can only be death immersed for so long, and then it affects you. When I started to have my own combat nightmares, I knew that I had had enough. Besides, I felt that I could make a greater contribution by moving larger systems around than sitting in an office doing individual psychotherapy (ala Matthew Dumont).

My anxiety about clinical practice was very high. I was very unhappy. I was very stressed. So when an administrative post in community health came about in 1990, I grabbed it. I applied for and was hired as the president and CEO for the Greater New Bedford Community Health Center, Inc. I was thrilled to get out of office practice and direct patient care in psychology and go into community health. I think that Matthew Dumont would have approved.

Eventually, after driving from Worcester to New Bedford for five years, we decided that this job was permanent and we should move. The year we moved, my mother became very ill and moved in with us. We packed up and sold her condo in Brookline, sold our house, and relocated to Dartmouth, Massachusetts, where two of our sons went to high school and our oldest son went into the army. This was a lot of transitional stuff.

We stayed in the New Bedford area until 2016. I quit my job at the health center in 2007 after a successful career building community health programs. (See appendix B.) I received many recognitions for my work, including having been voted the *New Bedford Standard Times* Man of the Year for 2006 and receiving a Certificate of Special Congressional Recognition offered by the Hon. Congressman Barney Frank. I had constructed a new, modern, state-of-the-art health center and expanded our patient services from five thousand persons to twenty-five thousand persons, representing about one-quarter of the city of New Bedford (the fourth largest city in Massachusetts). I enlarged the staff from thirty-six to almost 250 employees. We took over much of a city block in downtown New Bedford. We created the first dental program for Medicaid recipients in southeastern Massachusetts and so forth (see appendix B).

During this time, many friends and relatives passed away. I had responsibility for many of them and for their funerals. My mentor and friend Rabbi Weisenberg passed away in 1991 just as I began my work at the GNBCHC. Auntie Rae passed away in Florida after a long battle with cancer in 2006. I flew back and forth to Florida during that time to manage her care. My best friend, Jim Forleo, passed away. Two of my close friends and fishing companions, Ray Sprindzunas and Charlie Barnes, PhD, passed away. My good neighbor and friend Steven Arsenault passed away and I was with him at his death. My three elderly cousins in Worcester passed away, and I took responsibility for their funerals and estates. My mother passed away after seven years in a nursing home, the same day I graduated from the Spertus College with a master of science in Jewish studies in Chicago and entered their doctoral program in 2008. My good colleague Revered Brad Sell passed away (the southeastern Massachusetts organization COAST gave me a lifetime achievement award in his name). I felt crushed by responsibilities, achievements, losses, illnesses, and recognitions. The entire course of a busy life. My obsessive anxiety returned in full force.

Then I got severe prostatitis. I wound up in hospital unable to urinate.

This time, I not only sought psychiatric help, but I found that I could not do my job. I resigned as CEO in 2007 to get out from under the stress and pursue my passion for Jewish studies, which concluded with my master of science in Jewish studies in 2008. The responsibilities of work, family, caring for friends and sick relatives passing the world, children leaving for the army and to college, and my own physical illnesses collapsed me. I had to go on a selective serotonin reuptake inhibitor for my obsessive anxieties.

Few who knew me realized what I was going through. It was severe and painful and interrupted my abilities to work and be the pater familius. My sons were very concerned and upset. My wife came close to divorcing me because of my kookiness.

A by-product of all this was that my lousy brain chemistry was corrected. That had a direct effect on my physical status as well. I lost my irritable bowel syndrome. My anxiety resolved. My obsessiveness resolved. My religiosity (not my spirituality) began to improve.

I have become a great devotee to neuroscience through these experiences. Without the proper brain chemistry, one can pray all they want to, but it might avail them not. That was my case. When combined with my intellectual studies on higher text criticism with a better brain chemistry and less obsessive anxiety, my religiosity decreased substantially. This my family appreciated well.

We joined a Conservative shul after I helped to close the Orthodox shul in our area. If you do not have a minyan, you do not have a shul. If anyone asks you to close a shul, say no. It was one of the worst experiences of my life. The board asked me to take charge of the closure because of my administrative and Judaic skills and the fact that it was just so painful for long-term members. I said yes out of communal duty. I do not know if I would do that again.

I taught higher text criticism at that new synagogue for six years. Overall, my anxiety about the practice of Judaism calmed down. That did not mean that I valued Judaism any less. It simply meant that I was less obsessed with the "do this and do that" part of Jewish practice (the Confucian stuff).

Being on the right medication and a much better path in life meant that when I was diagnosed with prostate cancer, I was much more able to handle the entire matter. In pre-op for that surgery in 2013, they discovered that I had aortic stenosis. Eleven months after radical prostate surgery, I had open-heart surgery to replace my valve in 2014. During that operation, they also discovered that I had a 90 percent blocked coronary artery and gave me a bypass graft at the same time that they gave me a new valve (like a two for one deal). Four years later, they discovered that I still had cells left over from the prostate surgery and that they were metastatic. In the pre-op for that problem, they discovered that I had a rare form of lung cancer. So I had lung surgery in 2018. Today, I am living with metastatic prostate cancer and going one day after the next.

While writing this book in 2019, I fell down the stairs and broke four bones in my left foot and broke my ankle. This required the implant of a titanium plate screwed into the ankle. I had to walk in a boot/cast for months and had six months of physical therapy. So, having been screwed, I also got the boot! But I did not break my head falling down the stairs. It could have been a real catastrophe.

Fortuitously, I was also able to save my Chihuahua, Bella, who has three legs due to cancer and whom I was carrying down stairs. Had I fallen another way, she could have been badly hurt or killed. Chance favored her too.

There are those who would say that there is someone looking out for me for me to have survived all these health challenges. I do not see evidence that there are facts to support that position. Rather, I think that "I was a victim of a series of accidents, as are we all."[60] I was fortunate. Probability was in my favor. It could have just as easily gone the other way.

Managing life in the health fast lane has been much easier. I no longer pray for recovery. My prayer is more "I hope that it will occur that I will survive these illnesses." I am not an avid prayer to a god that I no longer believe in to intervene in the lives of people and change the laws of physics on their behalf. And yet I still allow prayers for wellness (meshebeyrach) to be said on my behalf at shul. It is like chicken soup. It couldn't hurt. I have still not ruled out the efficacy of prayer to improve people's character. I also have not ruled out the collective unconscious. So, meshebeyrachs couldn't hurt.

My ability to manage major stressors is a result of growing older and wiser, the proper brain chemistry, a reduced religious anxiety, reduced stressors, and the Taoist/Zen attitude of letting things take their course. I am still striving to get good at this.

These days, when I run into conflict, I generally remove myself. That happened religiously when we moved to New York. I have been in the Jewish community as a leader much of my life. My experience in our new community made me regret leaving our Jewish community of so many years in Massachusetts. But we moved for the right reasons—to be close to our children and grandchildren. That part of the move worked.

In 2018, Debbie and I tried a Reform shul in New York. We learned that we are not Reform. We now have been members of Orthodox shuls, Conservative shuls, and Reform shuls, which gives us a large spectrum of participation in and direct understanding of Jewish denominations. But even with significant Jewish communal experience and graduate education, I am still a lost soul … an apikoros (heretic) to the traditionalists and one who is concerned with orthopraxis to the progressives. I am an iconoclast in so many things in my life.

We are currently in a Conservative shul, and I started a chavurah. These have been rewarding so far. Of course, one always must reserve judgment on everything new (or old). It reminds me of the story of the person who jumped from the one hundredth story of the Empire State building. Passing fifty floors, the person said, "Well, so far so good."

I am much happier with my evolved theology. I am not as happy about our practice. You see, despite everything, I still believe in the Jewish people. I honor my ancestors and do not wish to abandon the millennia of the Jewish journey through time. So, what to hold onto and what to give up? This is a problem of ongoing concern and a part of my continuing journey.

Clearly to me, I am not comfortable with either end of the spectrum.

As an equal opportunity criticizer, I do not appreciate the rejection of the Halakah (other than the moral law) I found in the Reform, and I have trouble with some Hasidim who hold a christology regarding their Rebbe to be the Maschiah. I want my Judaism to respect the Halakah but not be so wedded to it that one cannot live a secular life either.

Ideologically, while I am an equal opportunity criticizer, it appears that in practice I am tending to the right, and in theology I am tending to the left. Oy!

I have learned so much about religion, Judaism, and denominationalism through the very broad experiences I have had. Besides the feeling of being a lost Jewish soul, I really do have a good grasp now on the pros and cons of the various denominations in Judaism, what people seem to want out of religion, and what I want. The far right of all religions seems to satisfy tribalistic, obsessive, and death-anxiety needs. The far right of religion (Hasidim) appears to me to satisfy the definition of cultism in its reverence for the Rebbe of each Hasidic dynasty. Whether it is Lev Tahar or Satmar or Breslov or Chabad, it seems to me that cultism in the form of Rebbeism is predominant and of concern. Yet, *Kol Yisrael averim zeh l' zeh* (All Israel is responsible, one for the other). Everyone must be at the table.

Fundamentalism is also characteristic of the far right in religions and is never any good. Fundamentalism is no good in Christianity, Judaism, Islam, Hinduism, or anything else. It is an anti-intellectual approach based on sets of beliefs and assumptions that are not open to investigation as to their validity or invalidity. They also do not lead to "love of one's fellow" but rather are exclusionary in their basic nature, in my humble opinion as an equal opportunity criticizer.

Over-ritualization is a disease that can also lead one out of this world. Ritual is valuable for all human activities and satisfies a whole set of needs at an emotional level. Some of these needs are benign, and some are detrimental to social and mental health. Ritual, being universal, is of obvious importance to social and psychological well-being if handled appropriately. If overdone, it can be obsessive and counter therapeutic. But I still appreciate many aspects of the services of the right based on their halachic authenticity.

On the left, the abandonment of ritual is problematic for me. The Enlightenment idea of the integrity and sovereignty of the individual had a deleterious effect on community, religion, faith, and ritual. In my own religion, one sees this in Humanistic Judaism, Reform Judaism, and Reconstruction Judaism. I will speak to this issue within my own religion, as I do not have the experience to speak to it within other religions except on an academic basis.

In 1885, the Reform held what became known as the Trefay Dinner (a non-kosher dinner) at which they announced their platform in Pittsburg, Pennsylvania. At that dinner, they served everything non-kosher that they could think of. The behavioral implications were to show that the Halakah (the codification of Jewish law) no longer held any sway for the Reform. Being children of the Enlightenment, only the individual sovereign self could determine what to observe and what not. Institutional religious law was abrogated by the Enlightenment. And nowhere was this more evident than in the Jewish Reform.

More than one hundred years later, the Reform accounts for some 30 plus percent of all American Jews. Yet the Reform is an anathema to the Orthodox, as the Orthodox are to the Reform. I expect that is not much different within other religious traditions on the right and the left of those traditions. From experience, I can say that a Reform Jew might experience Jewish Orthodoxy as something from another planet, and so too vice versa. The Reform Jew is lost in an Orthodox environment, and an Orthodox Jew is equally dislocated in a Reform environment. That has been my experience and understanding. It is not a good thing in my opinion.

Something is gained by the sovereignty of the individual, and something is lost. Untrained congregants cannot make theological decisions based on what they feel and not what they intellectually understand. An untrained and Halachically uneducated Jew cannot be expected to make informed decisions regarding Jewish law (or Jewish ritual observance). Neither is it fair to assume that dictums millennia old can all apply to the modern era. The question is, What is worth preserving and what is not? This is a critical dilemma that should not be left to the uninformed. It is much better to be critical of things you know about and have examined rather than to be critical about things you have not studied and know little about.

My discomfort with Jewish Orthodoxy stems from its fundamentalism, misogyny, homophobia, and xenophobia. I expect that I might feel the same way about the far right of many other religions. My discomfort with Jewish Orthodoxy also is based on my theological perspective about my definition of God. As is apparent by now in this text, I reject the idea of God as a noun that intervenes in the affairs of people, in favor of a definition of God as a verb that is the full working of the universe in all its complexities, randomness, and evolutionary truths.

Of course, it is hard to pray to a verb. We are trained to pray to some form of a noun god. Our language shows our propensity to envision god as "our Father," "our King," to "save us," "protect us," "grant us peace," and so on. This is the prayer language that envisions god as a noun. It might seem less satisfying to say, "May it come to pass that so and so will get well." To whom or what is this addressed? To the laws of physics? To mathematical probabilities? It is hard to offer up prayer to the universe because we, unlike Buddhists and Taoists, for example, are not trained to think in grand uncertainties. Prayer flags waving in the wind offering up prayer to the universe are foreign indeed to Western people. Getting beyond the concept of god as a noun to god as a verb is not easy.

So, if the Bible is not of divine origin, as Friedman suggests, and is rather of human production, where does that leave us? Does it invalidate Judaism? To quote Friedman as we have to introduce this chapter, "What are we to do with this knowledge?"

What, indeed! This is a lifetime's journey. My conclusion is that the human origin of the text does not diminish its importance to the Jewish people, its depth or richness as literature, or the wisdom of the sages of blessed memory. The matter does require the resolution of cognitive dissonance. From the perspective of pedagogy, should we continue to teach legends and myths as if they were facts?

My summary of learning from Friedman is this: *"The truth will make you free, but first it will make you miserable."*

An End of Faith, Religion, Terror, and the Future of Reason by Sam Harris, 2004

> There can be no doubt that religious faith remains a
> perpetual source of human conflict.[61]

Sam Harris will speak his truth. Harris is a neuroscientist/philosopher who is interested in the areas of belief and disbelief. He wrote *An End of Faith, Terror, Religion, and the Future of Reason.* I consider this book groundbreaking, and it occupies a spot in my pantheon of fourteen books.

My middle son introduced me to the Sam Harris's book. He knew that I was still a religious Jew but one who also could appreciate the intellectual integrity of atheism. I think he appreciated my struggles with religion. He had asked me to write a Tzavah to him and his brothers answering the question of how a religious Jew could also appreciate atheism. It took me over a year to produce anything cogent.

My Tzavah never seemed to satisfy my kids though. It didn't really satisfy me either. I was still working in New Bedford and had many conflicts personally, at work and religiously. Reading Sam Harris was actually somewhat clarifying.

Sam Harris has been known as one of the Four Horsemen of the Apocalypse that included the anti-religionist atheists of himself, Daniel Dennett, Richard Dawkins, and the late Christopher Hitchens. These are atheists who have no use for religion and see it as a negative influence on humankind. This is a theme explored in *An End of Faith*. Harris carefully and surgically dissects religious texts of the three Abrahamic faiths to explore the negative influence of religion on the human species. He spends a lot of his time in the book on Islam and its scripture, the Quran. But neither the Hebrew nor Christian scriptures escape dissection either.

The Hebrew scripture is certainly violent, prejudiced, and genocidal. However, those characteristics are not upheld by the Rabbinic Judaism of today or by the sages of the Talmud of yesteryear. It refers to eras gone by for millennia. No one practices the religion of biblical Israel over Rabbinic Judaism any more(with the possible exceptions of Karaites).

The Quran's prescriptions, according to Harris's examination of the text, recommend some very nasty things to do to law violators and infidels. The Hebrew scripture's punishments for various crimes can also be pretty gruesome. The Christian scripture, outside of the statement from the Hebrew scripture, to "love your neighbor as yourself," is not particularly filled with love (especially toward Jews). The Christian scripture deals with slavery by stoically telling slaves to be good slaves and to obey their masters (Ephesians 65–9). It tells women to be silent before men (1 Timothy 1:11 and 12). The Christian and Islamic texts are concerned for the poor, but so is the jealous and violent God of the Hebrew scripture, as well (see Proverbs 31:9).

Sam Harris, like his colleagues Dennett, Dawkins, and Hitchens, is an equal opportunity criticizer when it comes to religion. They are right in so many ways that I believe that *An End of Faith* may be one of the most important books of the twenty-first century, written to an American nation that is at least as religious regarding Christianity as Saudi Arabia is to Islam. But *An End of Faith* is also not totally on point, in my opinion.

While the texts of the three Abrahamic faiths are central to those religions, the Talmud brought the religion of biblical Israel into the first through sixth centuries CE, numerous papal bulls and encyclicals, the Protestant Reformation, Vatican II, including "Nostra aetate," and so forth updated the understanding of the New Testament and Christianity as a whole. The Hadith added to understandings of the original Quranic text. While there are those who would like to practice Judaism as a biblical religion, Christianity as a first- to fourth-century religion, and Islam as a seventh-century religion, there have been updates that allow each religion to function in some modern way, more or less.

The anti-religionist atheists complaint that religion has been the cause of wars and suffering throughout the history of humankind is also a concept taken to task by Karen Armstrong in her book *Fields of Blood*. A thesis always seems to have an antithesis (and, one hopes, a synthesis).

I subscribe to the idea that you cannot offer myths and legends as if they were fact and get away with that forever. This is especially true if those legends are violent in content. Each of the texts does exactly that ... offers myths and legends as facts without anything other than tautological proofs.

Many people, myself included, grew up on myths and legends presented to us by parents and teachers as if they were facts. The problem is that when one confronts the truth and learns that those myths and legends were myths and legends, one can go into cognitive dissonance and indeed get angry at feeling betrayed by prior generations we trusted. Noah and his flood is the Sumerian story of Gilgamesh. It is highly improbable and without secondary evidence in archaeology or history to prove that 603,550 Israelite men at arms and their families (about three million people) lived in the Sinai Desert for forty years before invading the land of Israel and committing genocide against the indigenous peoples there. A total of three million people leaving a society of five million people and staying in a desert for forty years is a preposterous belief. Yet millions (if not billions) believe it. It is equally preposterous that the sun stopped moving so that Joshua could fight longer. That is, first of all, a geocentric concept of astrophysics and, second, a preposterous idea given the fact of gravity and Newton's three laws of motion. Similarly, people do not return from the dead, nor are there sheep that have golden fleece, and the earth did not shake *because* the Buddha touched it. Epic legends are culturally and symbolically important, but we must not mistake legends for realities.

The texts themselves bear witness to the fact that it was written by human beings more for political reasons than for anything else. Every culture has its epic legends. There is nothing wrong with that. There is something wrong with telling children that epic legends are truths. Achilles was not killed just by an arrow in his foot, nor did Medusa exist with a head whose hair was snakes. Sirens did not affect the journey of Odysseus, and thunder does not come from Thor's hammer. These are legends and myths. They are stories that might provide morality tales, but they are not truth statements.

Truth statements are based on second-source evidence, on data, on historical literature and archaeological findings. Truth statements can be proven or disproven, and verified or falsified. Truth statements can be investigated, and those investigations can be replicated to show their validity and reliability. Truth statements do not violate the laws of physics, if they are indeed truth statements. Truth statements, if indeed true, can be used to predict other truths.

A source that says something is true because that source says it is true is telling us a tautological statement, not a truth statement. To say that Moses received the Torah on Sinai from God because the Hebrew scripture says so is a circular argument. So, when we confront these religious issues as adults, we can experience cognitive dissonance, anger, and disillusionment.

That may be the source of anger for some anti-religionist atheists. Of course, the other issue is atheism itself as an intellectual response to the matter of the existence of God.

I do not care whether you subscribe to the ontological proof of[62] god, the cosmological proof[63] of god, or any other proof of god. The concept of a divine being that created the universe is unknowable and ineffable to human beings, and that god interferes in the laws of physics on behalf of certain people is an illogical and unprovable position. To every proof of god's existence with the qualities stated above, there is a disproof. Belief is neither science nor proof of a truth statement. Such are in the realm of metaphysics and not physics. And any fool can believe anything. People have believed that the earth is flat and that the sun revolves around the earth.

Take as an example the Great Flying Spaghetti Monster (GFSM), now adopted as a real religion by certain states in the world. GFSM devotees wear colanders on their heads and believe(so they tell us) that people are held on the earth not by gravity but by the spaghetti tentacles of the GFSM. Is this any more preposterous than the belief that the prophetic golden tablets could only be read with special glasses like reading materials, or that the Japanese islands were formed by a god dropping drops of the ocean into the sea from his spear, or that thunder is caused by Thor's hammer, or that when you die, you must pay the boatman to take you across the River Styx to the afterlife, or that the phoenix bird survives death in fire to become resurrected, or that the Aztec sun god requires the blood of slaves and captives to ensure a good harvest? How about a man dying and being resurrected? How about a wafer that becomes the body of a godhead and wine that becomes his blood, and that when one consumes these, they commune with that deity in a process that appears to outsiders to be a cannibalistic ritual? Billions of people have believed in one or more of these stories as facts over time.

Nicholas Wade explored the human need for such stories in his book the *Faith Instinct*. Sigmund Freud examined these issues as a part of his analysis of the unconscious.

Numerous authors and books have tried to understand the human need for religion, myth, legends, and ritual. It is a human need as evidenced by billions of people believing in religion and its legends as facts around the world and throughout human history. The noted author James Campbell has written about the nature and use of myth in the human experience and has helped evaluate this need in human beings. The psychoanalyst Carl Jung also wrote extensively on this subject in his famous text *Man and His Symbols*, for example.

Having needs for stories, needs for protection from a hostile world, and needs for order are not the same as *needing* truth and facts. Science needs truth, data, and facts. Religion needs beliefs and faith on their own face value. This was St. Thomas Aquinas's problem in trying to reconcile faith and reason. He decided that there were two kinds of truths, one by faith and one by reason. Of course, as a churchman, when he was in doubt, he defaulted to faith. Science defaults to reason. Resolving the two can lead to cognitive dissonance.

Cognitive dissonance can be resolved (or not) in a number of ways once truth meets fiction:

1. One can accept the new information that makes sense versus the old information and reframe our understanding of the facts.
2. One can retain their acceptance of the old information and reject the new facts.
3. One can remain conflicted.
4. One can deny both the new and old information and become an atheist.

Whatever the choice, the choice selection can be painful.

I have witnessed this all too often with friends, students, and colleagues. As with *Who Wrote the Bible?*, the anti-religionist atheists stir up things that we have either chosen not to confront or just simply let go over a lifetime. The feeling of betrayal is deep and real. "Why didn't my father tell me this?" "I feel betrayed by my teachers." "Does the rabbi know this?" or "You just do not understand." I even saw a student kick a chair across a classroom in frustration when confronting the implications of higher text criticism. Dissonance can be very emotional. These are all questions stated with great concern that I have heard regarding learning that truth and legend are not the same thing. "The truth will make you free, but first it will make you miserable."

Is religion the "opiate of the masses" as Karl Marx suggested,[64] or is it an anchoring for the masses among a sea of things that we can never understand? It is probably wrong to believe that religion is the cause of every evil. There is plenty of evil in the human species to go around. Science and technology can create their own evil—to wit, the atomic bomb.

All these questions came to trouble me too. This was especially true during my studies at Hebrew College's Me'ah program (2003–2005), later at Spertus College in my master of science in Jewish studies program

(2005–2008), and when I was in their doctoral program (2008–2011). Clearly, Jewish studies in the secular world of Judaism brings forth these questions. At Me'ah, the first text we studied was *Who Wrote the Bible?* I never studied Sam Harris at Spertus College, but I should have. The result for me would have been the same: legend is not fact.

Not only are legends and myths not facts, but we should not teach them as such. When we condition young children to believe in Noah's ark, and then in later life they find out that such an ark and such a flood never happened, they can become disillusioned and go into cognitive dissonance. One way to teach these stories is to identify that they are myths and legends as metaphors to support the moral messages being highlighted in the stories. I know that such a pedagogy/andragogy is necessary. Without it, the cognitive dissonance will continue, and we will perpetuate the fractured historical account of Jewish history.

I cannot speak for my sons, but I do suspect that a part of what distanced them from Traditional Observant Judaism were the issues posed when they found out that the myths were not true and had been presented to them in their childhoods as facts (in Hebrew school, camps, etc.). What I failed to do well was to communicate that the Torah text is not just narrative (aggadah) but also a code of jurisprudence (halachah) that was revolutionary in its time in the ancient Near East.

Dissonance is universal. I have been admonished not to tell my grandchildren that Santa Claus is not real. I probably should not tell them the truth about the tooth fairy either. When they do find out the truth, they will be disappointed. And they very well may hand the falsehoods on to their children as well.

I have heard it said, but I do not know where to attribute this, that there are two great pillars of secularism, Darwin and evolution by natural selection and the documentary hypothesis or higher text criticism. I would add two more legs to the chair to include the Heisenberg uncertainty principle and Gödel's incompleteness theorem. I suppose that Sam Harris would add neuroscience. But I will not. I think that it is enough to recognize the effects of evolutionary theory, higher text criticism, Heisenberg's uncertainty principle, and Gödel's incompleteness theorem. By the time you are done with understanding these four pillars, voila, you are secular.

And indeed that has been my journey. I have gone from a devoutly religious person to a devoutly religious secular person (ala Edgar Bromfield and his book *Why Be Jewish, A Testament*). How confusing for those who love and know me.

I respect the traditions of my people that have been acquired over millennia. I respect the fact that many people have died rather than give up these traditions, practices, rituals, and legends as fact. I have significant trouble being disloyal to my people and to their history. And yet it is clear to me that our traditions are based on the misconceptions that legends are indeed facts. Fairy tales have been told in every religion over millennia. So, what is one to do?

My children know the truth. They know that the traditions are based on epic legends. Can we build respect for the epic legends while maintaining our skepticism based in secularism and truth? I believe that the answer is complicated, but yes. But this approach requires recognizing that the Torah text is a bifold story of both aggadah and halachah. Taken in this manner, it can make more sense.

This is why I believe that Sam Harris is one of the most important authors in the twenty-first century to date. Yes, he seems angry. Yes, he is an atheist. Yes, he is a scientist first and foremost. He brings to light a truth. And, as I have pointed out before, "the truth will make you free, but first it will make you miserable."[65]

So, in the end, I had to revise my own Judaism both through Sam Harris, through Hebrew College, Spertus College, and through my own studies to understandings my children were aware of long before I was.

God, as I understand the term, is a mental construct. The Torah and the Abrahamic scriptures, as I understand then within their own contexts, are of human construction. Legends and myths can be important to illuminate moral truths but are not always facts. The scriptures are more political documents and literature as much as statements of religious truth and value claims. So, now that Julius Wellhausen, Sigmund Freud, Yehezkel Kaufman, Richard Elliot Freedman, Sam Harris and his associates, and many others have opened up Pandora's religious box, what are we to do?

I think that the answer may lie in *Why Be Jewish, A Testament* by Edward Bronfman. Bronfman created "Birthright Israel," in which Jewish kids are sent to Israel at his expense to experience the homeland. Bronfman wrote this book when he knew he was dying and wanted to leave a statement of legacy. He did a great job. The book explains secular Judaism in a meaningful and dramatic way. I identified with every section of the book.

Clearly, I have given up the concept of an ineffable God as a noun who created the universe and intervenes in it on behalf of certain people. This is a primitive concept of God. Rather, I have moved to the concept that "everything is God," which is the concept of Spinoza, Einstein, and the book by the same title by Jay Michaelson. Yes, this has roots in Kabbalah and in Hasidism. Yes, this holds elements of pantheism and even panentheism. But it is a concept that more closely matches my concerns today than ever before.

God, for me, is a concept of mind. It is an expression through a word to describe awe and trembling before the vastness of the universe and its processes. God does not intervene in the laws of physics because god is the laws of physics.[66]"Things happen as they must, not as they should" or how we wish that they would.[67] But it is not wrong to be in awe of the processes of the universe. It is wrong to ask that God intervene on our particular behalf.

This brings us once again to the issue of theodicy. Theodicy, as I have noted before, is the single most important question to be addressed by philosophy today (in my humble opinion). Theodicy is the question of how can a merciful god allow evil to exist. The answer is, it cannot. In that case, god cannot be a noun but must be a verb if it is anything at all. *God is the sum total of the universe and its processes.* If it is a noun, then the theodicy question remains operative and can never be solved.

The End of Faith combined with *Who Wrote the Bible?* are therefore two of the most formative books for me and my philosophy. The Orthodox *Siddur Kol Yaakov* may be the reservoir of Jewishness, but it is not the reservoir of objective truth. The Siddur is critically important for religio-cultural reasons and not for truth statements. That Siddur contains the journey of our people over millennia. That is a large part of its value to me.

Edgar Bronfman's solution within secular Judaism, proposed within his book *Why Be Jewish, A Testament*, seems to me to be different from the attempts of the Reform to revise Judaism. Secular Judaism is not Reform Judaism. The Reform has taken the position that Judaism is not a reflection of a people but that Judaism is a religion like other religions. Bronfman seems to see Judaism as the religion of the Jewish people.

I would suggest that Judaism has never been monolithic but that all of the Judaisms have been Jewish. That is because it is the Jewish people of which we are a part. We are not Reform Jews, or Conservative Jews, or Orthodox Jews, or Hasidic Jews, or socialist atheist Jews. We are the Jewish people who hold within them various theological and political positions but are still one people, one nation. While it may be important to define our relationship to God, it is also important to define our relationship to the corpus of Jewish law and literature, to the traditions of the Jewish people, to the history of the Jewish people, and to the land of Israel as the national homeland of the Jewish people.

When we make ourselves into a religion only, we lose the very nature of what it means to be Jewish.

Finally, conclusions I have from reading Sam Harris is that *it is a sin to lie to others, but it is an even greater sin to lie to ourselves.* And "the truth will make you free, but first it will make you miserable."

Book 14

The Drunkard's Walk—How Randomness Rules Our Lives by Leonard Mlodinow, 2013

> My mother always warned me not to think I could predict or control the future.[68]

I came to Leonard Mlodinow through his books with Deepak Chopra and with Stephen Hawking. I thought that he was not only a good writer but also really smart. I was teaching philosophy at Bristol Community College in Fall River, Massachusetts, when I read *The Drunkard's Walk*. I incorporated it into my teaching of philosophy.

What I like about Leonard Mlodinow is that he appears to be an atheist who is unabashedly Jewish. The son of survivors of the Holocaust, he is a theoretical physicist who wrote *The Grand Design* with Stephen Hawking. He also wrote a very well done book with Deepak Chopra called *War of the Worldviews* in which they lay out cases for metaphysics versus physics. But our focus herein will be on his book on randomness, *The Drunkard's Walk*.

Mlodinow tells us that he came to randomness through his parents' reports of how they survived the concentration camps … by chance. Many survivors will say the same thing. They survived by chance and chance alone. Not luck, mind you, but chance. Luck indicates that there might be something special about the person who is *lucky*. In the Holocaust, people survived because of random probabilities.

Why did some scoundrels survive and other great leaders and Talmud scholars perish?[69] It is improper to suggest that God had a design in which this would occur for purposes known only to the deity. Such a deity needs psychotherapy. Why did a million and a half innocent Jewish children perish? What sins did they commit? And even if you believe that there is national punishment of the Jewish people for sins, what sins were so great that the fires of the Holocaust were just reward? What kind of deity takes revenge on children for the sins of parents multi-generationally? What kind of vile deity is this?

As the reader can tell, I have a good deal of anger over this. Once I decided that God could not be held accountable for the process of the universe, then my anger at God was mitigated, and my anger at human beings increased. I did go through a long period of anger at God for the Holocaust and all of the other abuses that the Jewish people have had to endure under both Christian and Muslim rule. That anger, in and of itself, turned me away from the concept of a benevolent deity who rules the universe toward the concept of God as the process of the universe itself.

As I went through my transition, I experienced my anger to make me appear like a crazed person at times. I was angry at God. I was angry at my parents and grandparents for deluding me. I was angry at my rabbis and Hebrew school teachers for not telling me the truth. I was angry at myself for my own religious stupidity and for trying to pass it on to another generation.

It is because I myself experienced cognitive dissonance that I had such compassion for those undergoing the process. Yet I continue to provoke people to confront truth and to question everything. As teacher, I stimulate dissonance. Sometimes I feel that this form of andragogy is cruel. Perhaps Vonnegut was right to point out that sometimes it is okay to lie to reduce suffering. The truth is a harsh master.

Well, I suppose that you could suggest that Satan is real and behind all evil and the Holocaust. But if there is a deity that allows Satan power over the righteous, one still has to question such a deity's motives. Theodicy will just not go away as long as God is a noun and has control over the universe and can make moral decisions that affect human beings and other living things.

Then there are the findings of mathematics and science that reveal the way the universe works. And it works in a random nature. That is a fundamental of quantum theory, of the Heisenberg uncertainty principle, and of physics itself. Einstein did not like that idea. He argued that God "does not play dice."[70] Hawking used to say that God not only plays dice but "throws them under the table" where you cannot see them.[71] Randomness is operative in the universe, and as such, we can predict things within probabilities and not much more. Beauty will save the world[72] (as Fyodor Dostoyevsky famously told us in *The Idiot*),[73] but statistics and probability rule the world. Certainly, randomness plays more of a part in our lives than we might have wished to admit.

And once again, here I am not discussing luck. Luck implies that there is some special quality about the lucky person that tips the scales in their favor. One might be fortunate but not lucky. We win things because of randomness and not because of luck or because of the selection of the deity.

I guess I would like to believe that you can nudge the scales of probability this way or that way and can increase the probability of success or not. "Chance favors only the prepared mind."[74] Preparation may increase the probability of a successful outcome, but to what degree? That degree might be less than the probabilities a random universe allows.

This concept is foreign, if not counterintuitive, to many people who desire the world to work according to principles of fairness and the reward of hard work. It is a disturbing concept. "What about cause and effect?" one might ask. Well, what about cause and effect? Can we predict that if x happens, 100 percent of the time y will occur? Can we know anything at 100 percent degree of confidence? We might like to think so. In fact, it makes us uncomfortable to believe that this is not the case. But it is not the case. We can predict within probable parameters and limits but not at a 100 percent degree of confidence. Certainty is beyond human control.

Human beings have great needs for the world to be certain. We are omnivores. But we also require animal protein. We are originally hunting animals as well as gatherers. Hunting animals need a high degree of certainty in order to hunt successfully. That is probably why Mother Nature gave prey camouflage in order to confuse predators and also gave mammal predators binocular vision and bilateral hearing to increase their ability to visually triangulate where their prey might be located. This balances the chances within the prey/predator relationship ratio. Predators like certainty better than uncertainty in their hunting behaviors.

When our world is uncertain, we make every attempt to make it certain. If our memory is spotty, for example, we fill in the blanks. This is reconstructed memory and the reason that it is very hard to depend on memory in a court of law. Certainly, the probability of accuracy goes up the more independent witnesses you can get to a single event. But the fact remains that our brains like certainty so much that we will fill in the blank areas of both recognition and memory to make us feel certain.

This is true in the case of religion and spirituality too. If our ancestors did not understand lightning, they made up a Zeus who threw lightning bolts. If they did not understand thunder, they made up Thor and his famous hammer. The world was dangerous and, without science, hard to understand (it is hard to understand with science). It is much better to go through a life of danger when you postulate a beneficent paternal deity who will take care of you. The problem is that, because of the concept of reciprocity, we postulate that the deity needs things from us to act beneficently toward us. It needs animal sacrifices, human sacrifices, obeying laws that can be brutal or inane, and prayer (which seems much more benign). These, it seems to me, are constructions of the mind formed to render the world controllable. And yet the world is not controllable but random.

Leonard Mlodinow tells us the math and tells us the concepts. His message is fairly simple. It is important to recognize how the world really works, and in that recognition, we may obtain *humility*. However great we evaluate our efforts toward our successes, we must be humble, because it could have gone the other way. In fact, it often goes the other way just by chance. Unfortunately, human beings tend to over-evaluate themselves, and humility is often not expressed as a virtue.

In this mathematical/philosophical position, there is a sense of giving up of control. This is very, very hard for human beings. If we do not have control, we attribute control to a deity. Control (and power) are deep concerns for humans and might be illusions.[75]

I want to spend a moment on the evolution of appeasement of the deity. As I stated above, our ancestors felt that sacrifices appeased the deity. In some cultures, it was postulated that the deity needed to be fed. In the Aztec and Mayan cultures, that food was human blood. In the ancient Near Eastern cultures, the food for the gods were animals and the fruits of the harvest. But giving something of value to us up to the deity was a universal form of appeasement that could encourage beneficence from that deity.

The Aztecs and Mayans went a bit overboard with this in the form of human sacrifice, which included removal of the heart while the victim was still conscious, decapitation, tying the victim into a ball or using the victim's head as a ball in the temple ball game courtyard, and cannibalism of the sacrificial victim. I suspect that there was a good amount of sadism in these sacrificial traditions. Some other cultures were a bit less cruel and just beheaded people before burning them up as sacrifices. Then some cultures also practiced child sacrifice. Were these religio-cultural issues or the expression of some deep-seated sadistic pathologies?

Jews make a big deal over the point that for modern Judaism(s), prayer has replaced agricultural and animal sacrifice. But this was only true after the Romans destroyed the Jerusalem temple and the Jews no longer could sacrifice there. And yet, even modern Orthodox and many Conservative Jews pray for the restoration of the temple in Jerusalem and the sacrificial cult of the Kohanim. It is one thing to remember the centrality of the cult to the national independence and self-determination of the Jewish people within an ancient Jewish state. It is another to suggest that modern people return to primitive sacrifice to a God who likes the aroma of burning flesh as the Torah tells us (Leviticus 1:13). Prayer substituting for sacrifice is an evolution toward the position where prayer is a vehicle to self-improvement ... meditation, if you will. That is a progression toward being much more civilized.

So, in my evolution as a person, I have abandoned the idea of restoration of the Jerusalem temple as the site of the sacrificial cult and hope instead for the restoration of a self-determining, independent Jewish state and national homeland of the Jewish people based on the concepts of survival, on justice as fairness, and as a Light unto the Nations through the exercise of moral behavior. Jerusalem and the Temple Mount are the symbolic centers of independent self-determination for the Jewish people. Whether in a third temple we should return the sacrificial cult to operation or stay with prayer as the substitute for sacrifice is a debate for a different forum.

This might be a utopian hope, for it cannot come about unless there is justice for all. And to have a Jewish state means by definition that there can never be a Jeffersonian democracy with Arabs, Christians, and Jews having equal votes. That will mean the destruction of the Jewish people by population demographics alone. And there is the exact conundrum of the modern State of Israel. There must be a two-state solution to the Israeli/Palestinian problem. What will Israeli democracy look like within Israel proper without a two-state solution? Can one have a Jeffersonian democracy where every citizen has one equal vote in a unique Jewish state? These are vexing considerations.

Maintaining Jewish continuity is a probability that I do not wish to evaluate. And if everything is indeed random, then I will hope that the gods of randomness will tip the scales of probability toward the well-being of all people, especially the Jewish people, who have contributed and lost so much to humanity over time.

Ultimately, my affinity to the concept of randomness and the role it plays in our lives is based on my own self-perception as a scientist. I still wish to believe in choice, but I understand that our choices are much more limited than we may have thought. Perhaps it is the *striving* that is important, rather than the outcome. Perhaps the journey is more important than the destination.

Randomness teaches us humility in the face of both success and failure. Indeed, there are probably more failures than successes. There are not necessarily catastrophes but rather learning opportunities. Or maybe it is just how things work. By effect of our actions, we might be able to move the results a little bit this way or that to some degree, but the overall outcome is less predictable.

"God's ways are not our ways," say some of my religious friends. This is a default answer when we just do not understand what is happening. I am not so special that I should enjoy divine intervention, nor am I so terrible that I should suffer diseases that have adversely affected my life. I did not need these "tests," and I doubt that God, all merciful and compassionate, would afflict someone this way just for a test or to get his jollies. Job did not need the tests, and neither did the millions who were incinerated in the Holocaust. I reject that form of thinking. Rather, I appreciate the phrase, "I am a victim of a series of accidents, as are we all."

My life-threatening illnesses, discussed above, are evidence of the randomness of the world and not the intervention of a deity who could act more compassionately but does not. God does not intervene in the laws of physics. The god that is everything is also the laws of physics. God is the laws of physics. And the way the world is set up, entropy is operative. All things tend to fall apart, and the universe tends toward absolute zero. This is the second law of thermodynamics. Everything that is complex becomes less organized. Everything that is alive will die. Can you be angry at a physical law of nature that is "blind, indifferent and unloving?"[76]

I could be angry at God if I felt that God intentionally created the universe in such a way that suffering is built in. I could be angry about the genetics behind my aortic stenosis heart disease, but I am not. I could be angry at my urologic surgeon for leaving cells behind. But I am not. I was just unfortunate. This is not a stoic position; it is an affirmation of my understanding of the way things work in this universe. If I felt that there was an intelligent entity that created natural laws so that people would get surreptitious diseases, suffer, and die, then I might be angry with good reason. But the evidence does not point in that direction.

Buddhist cosmology assumes that the universe is infinite. Suffering is just built into the universe. It is the way things are. Buddhists give themselves much more opportunity for control by assuming that suffering is caused by attachment and that nonattachment is a method to resolve suffering. In some ways, this is a sophist idea. Sophism says that nothing really exists outside of our minds. While this might make our approach to suffering somewhat easier to understand and bear, it is also not the entire story. It is a helpful position but an incomplete one.

"Everything happens as it must, not as it should"[77]in accordance with the laws of physics/nature. Things happen randomly. We can only describe these events through mathematics and probabilities. You can rail against the facts of life, but it will avail you not. Or, you can accept the way things are, change what you can, hope for a good outcome, and try to do your best under the circumstances in which you find yourself. I feel that other positions toward suffering waste our precious time and mental energy. Better to assume a position in which you do less harm to yourself and others and use the little time that you have to best effect. To do otherwise is to squander a precious gift of the universe, self-consciousness.

This is just all a part of my journey. I think that it is all "striving toward" rather than "getting there" that is important. Life is a journey and not an outcome. You can move the probabilities a little this way or a little that way, but you cannot change the course of your life through effort alone. Probability must favor you, and that happens in some random way that we still do not fully understand. The best one can do is to do their best. The rest is up to the universe, which ticks along on its own course and governed by its own laws.

Recently, my surgeon commented on how many life-threatening illnesses I have overcome in the past number of years. He said that I reminded him of Private Ryan (from the film *Saving Private Ryan* by Steven Spielberg). He asked me, "So, Stu, have you been a good man?"

This was the question Private Ryan asked his wife about himself toward the end of the film, given that his dying captain in WWII had told him, "Earn this" (referring to his rescue). Virtually everyone else sent to find Private Ryan died in that rescue. My physician meant, Had I earned overcoming cancer and heart disease by leading a good life? Had God favored me?

I have tried to be a good man. My career of helping people has been the life of one I would consider as a good man. In small and larger ways, I have *striven* to be a good man. I rescued a pigeon with a broken wing. I helped a tired deer cross a large lake. I prevented a friend from committing suicide. I rejected the seductive advances of a colleague's wife. I volunteered for sixteen years to lead Rosh Hashanah services at a Jewish nursing home. I took care of my mother and my aunt when they were sick and dying. I organized the burials for cousins who had no one else to be interested. I financially and personally helped my cousin and his family when he was in need and dying. I closed a friend of mine's medical practice when he was dying and could no longer take care of patients. I saved a man's life who had been injured in a wilderness area. I rescued dogs and ministered to them when they needed palliative care. I offered my professional services in my community as a volunteer without thought of remuneration. I coached Little League for my sons and attended all of their games, sometimes running between three different fields at the same time. I taught a blind teenager how to play guitar as a kindness. I saved a patient's life at some risk to myself. I told the truth and remained ethical, even when it was hard to do so or meant my tenure in a job. I stood up for social justice through action and not just talk. I assisted my students when they needed help and/or encouragement. Tens of thousands of people received health care because of what I accomplished professionally. *I raised three good men.*

Equally, I was no saint either. I have had a quick wit and sometimes cruel mouth. I have a temper. Sometimes I lied and embellished. I was not always the present husband and father my family needed. Sometimes my ambition overcame my altruism. Sometimes, my altruism was just the sublimation of hostility. I can be lazy and avoidant. I might have given more to charities. At times, I ate and drank too much. Much of the time, I was my own worst critic. I do not suffer fools lightly. I can be aggressive. I can be intolerant.

But I never cheated on my wives. I did not steal. I never physically harmed another human being (other than in martial arts practice, and even then, I controlled myself).

I believe that, on balance, I have striven to be a good man. But I do not believe that my being good or bad have anything to do with my recovery from cancer, heart disease, or physical trauma. Those are random occurrences about which my life and ethics had no bearing. As it is said in *Pirke Avot*, "It is not within our power to understand the suffering of the righteous or the prosperity of the wicked."[78] And to quote Kurt Vonnegut again, "I was a victim of a series of accidents, as are we all."

I do not wish the reader to assume that I am a fatalist. Fate implies direction, as does *destiny*. I do not see that in the universe. Things happen as they have according to the natural laws of physics and not how we might wish they would.[79] I have a resolve not to try to adjust the universe to me but to adjust me to the universe. Struggling against the way things are is an endeavor that wastes time, and time is about all we have in a universe that is "blind, indifferent and unloving."[80] We have the opportunity to confront the facts of such a universe by being aware, involved, and loving. We can be empathetic to the plight of others and actively involved to help reduce suffering. I do not think that is a waste of time.

While there are few choices really available to us, we can try to choose awareness over unawareness, compassion over indifference, and caring over non-caring. Through those choices, which require conscious attention, we might improve the quality of our own lives and the lives of all other living things.

Understanding randomness can have a downside, just as understanding that there are limits on free will. That downside may be existential despair. Thoreau said that "the mass of men lead lives of quiet desperation."[81] Camus told us that "there is but one truly serious philosophical problem, and that is suicide."[82]

I believe that there are other aspects of life that can offset existential despair. Camus reveals this in *The Myth of Sisyphus*[83]in concluding, "The secret I am seeking lies hidden in a valley full of live trees, under the grass and the cold violets, around an old house that smells of wood." *JB* told us something similar in stating that "I would not sleep here if I could, except for the little green leaves in the wood and the wind on the water."[84]

Existential despair must be the servant of awe, thankfulness, and hope if we are to survive. Those three elements are my definition for spirituality.

The point is to live life. The Torah tells us "chose life."[85]Camus tells us that "the point is to live."[86] Living life, even with all its absurdities, is a great gift that the universe has given us. To waste it on hostility, aggression, and indifference is a sin that many of us commit.

So, rather than leading us into existential despair, appreciating how the world works, how random it can be, can provide us with what Heschel called "radical amazement."[87] Understanding randomness need not lead us into despair but rather into humbleness and appreciation. That appreciation should be in the here and now. Living life in anticipation of a hypothetical afterlife seems to me to be a gross waste of precious time and effort. Appreciate it now. Live it now. Too soon it will be over. This is the spirituality that comes from awe and the recognition of our own finite nature.

While randomness obviously rules our lives, human effort may be able to move things a bit this way or that way. I am not advocating that we have total free will. I do not believe that. I think that things are much more determined unconsciously than that (see Charles Brenner's book) by the unconscious mind, by genetics, and by our socio-cultural development. But one thing I can tell you from experience, the burdens and stressors of life take their toll.

I have seen too many of my colleagues burn out and leave the field. That happened to me too. So by 2007, I was fighting both physical and mental collapse. I did not feel that I could do my job anymore due to physical and emotional afflictions. I resigned my job to do graduate work in Jewish studies at Spertus College in Chicago. That was a good move for me. One can get to such a point of fatigue, even if one is careful.

I did get my master of science in Jewish studies in 2008. The next day, I entered the doctoral program at the school, and that night my mother passed away in Massachusetts. I really regretted not being with her when she passed.

I decided to drop out of the doctoral program. I had moved on from the need to formally continue my studies at the doctoral level. I would and did continue to strive on my own. Besides, during this time, I was facing a series of life-threatening challenges, including having prostate cancer and heart disease requiring open-heart surgery.

I did continue to work using my new credentials and older learning to assist Jewish communities that needed to merge their organizations for cost concerns. I also served as COO for the PACT program, sometimes referred to as the "domestic arm" of Partners in Health under the Brigham and Women's Hospital and the Harvard Medical School. I was laid off at BWH in 2010 and developed my consulting practice and adjunct teaching. My children were getting married, pursuing their own careers, and having children of their own.

Debbie's father passed away in 2010, and her mother developed Alzheimer's disease during this period. We moved her mother to a nursing home near us in 2014. She passed away in 2016. About a month later, I was called back to a community that I had merged in 2012 to be their CEO. With Debbie's mother's passing, we were free to move to New York to be closer to children and grandchildren. I took an apartment in Pennsylvania to serve as CEO of the Jewish Community Alliance of Northeastern Pennsylvania. I then joined Debbie in New York, where we bought a home and I semiretired. I was able at seventy-one years old to get a teaching job at a SUNY community college, teaching philosophy classes and world religions. I had begun teaching philosophy at Bristol Community College in Fall River, Massachusetts, in 2011. I thought that was pretty cool for an old guy.

In 2018, I had lung surgery in NYC. Today, I am still living with cancer. I continue to teach, both at college and in the Jewish community. In 2019, I fell down stairs and broke five bones in my left foot and ankle in a break that my surgeon told me he had not seen before. I am learning how to walk again.

Life's challenges never stop. One time, I asked my father, "When does it stop?" (referring to the stress of life).

"When you lie down in the dirt," he answered. Life just keeps happening. Through it all, my wife reminds me that we keep landing on our feet.

I do have a conclusive takeaway from Mlodinow, however. It is a similar takeaway that I got from reading Sheldon Kopp's works as well. Power and control are illusions. Life is a set of random occurrences over which we have little, if any, control.

Vonnegut was right; "I was a victim of a series of accidents, as are we all." Life is something that happens, and one must "flow with the oil." The boundary of my control has ended at my skin, as the ancient Chinese expression goes.

Total personal agency is most probably an illusion. Free will is a more limited option than we might wish it to be.

As for myself, my superego is pretty large and unforgiving. It is a tragic flaw in my personality. So, what did I learn from Leonard Mlodinow and my life at the time I discovered him? I learned "not to think I could predict or control the future." One can be humble in the face of that understanding, but *randomness still does not remove from you the obligation to strive to be a better person.*

I did my best with what I had to work with. I hope that those whom I offended forgive me and those whom I have helped will remember me kindly.

AFTERWORD

I want the reader to understand that, in my world, learning never ceases.

The books I have cited are certainly not my whole library. Many reference volumes, novels, poetry, and other genre fill my shelves. My total library today, after many purges through moving, consists of only about seven hundred or so volumes. This is probably the least number of volumes I have maintained in a long time.

I have not read anything in the past seven years that has affected me as significantly as the fourteen books I mentioned here. I have read important books, such as *Why Be Jewish, a Testament* by Edgar Bronfman, *The Cave and the Light* by Arthur Herman, and *The Order of Time* by Carlo Rovelli, all of which I consider very valuable. I have not read any of the recent books on the one whose name must not be mentioned, and I do not intend to. So, we will see what comes along.

My books are my precious friends. This exercise has been great in terms of cutting to the chase. Who knows what I might pick if I were to do the exercise again in a decade. Perhaps more reading and learning will lead me to other conclusions. Who knows? That is why we have something called model-dependent reality! Both openness of mind and a sense of healthy skepticism are tools in one's philosophical toolbox. I keep those tools readily at hand.

And you, dear reader, may wish to try this exercise for yourself.

THE SUM AND
SUBSTANCE OF IT ALL

I wish to summarize what my journey has meant to me and how these books have illuminated that journey. A technique I use in teaching is one of closure of a Gestalt by asking students to say what they took away from that particular class at its end. Here is the summary of my takeaways from this exercise:

1. "Nevertheless, that wasp killed four big men and converted a large powerful car into a heap of scrap."[88]

A person can make a difference, even a slight one. To quote Rabbi Tarfon, "It is not incumbent upon you to complete the work; yet, you are not free to desist from it"[89] (Pirke Avot, Mishnah 2, chapter 16). And I believe that we have an obligation to make whatever difference we can toward the relief of suffering and increase of well-being. We need to strive to make our efforts toward good and not selfishness or harm to others. I learned from *Wasp* *the power* of something small being able to affect the destiny of something much larger ... *of an individual to effect change*, either for good or not. These ideas have directed my life's work and personal mission.

2. "So much of what goes on in our minds is unconscious." [90]

I learned about the power of unconscious determinism from *An Elementary Textbook of Psychoanalysis*. Over time, I have added to that concept through my studies of neuroscience. I have come to believe that free will is not as self-determinative as we might like to believe. We are the end results of our genetic and biological histories, our psychological histories, and our sociological circumstances. Where those spheres of influence (bio-psycho-social) intersect together is us. Take away any of those systems, and we are not us any longer.

And most of this is below the level of our conscious awareness. Our nervous systems work very fast and between the neuro-initiation, and our feelings of awareness are many milliseconds. We are aware of what has taken place in our minds that is below the level of conscious awareness and which has already happened in the past. Full conscious determinism is probably more an illusion than a reality.

Behavior rests on factors we are not fully aware of.

3. "Therefore, hardness and stiffness are the companions of death. And softness and gentleness are the companions of life."[91]

I learned from the *Tao Te Ching* the value of quietism and letting things take their course. I also recognize how hard a task this is to accomplish, as long as you are trying to accomplish it. It is when one stops trying to accomplish things that the world is left to proceed as it must.

My conclusion from reading Lao Tzu is a question: ***How can one strive while letting go of striving and outcomes?*** It is a puzzlement.

4. "If god is good, He is not god. If god is god, He is not good. Take the even, take the odd. I would not sleep here if I could, except for the little green leaves in the wood and the wind on the water."[92]

I learned from *JB* (and from the book of Job) that *theodicy is a major issue* in theology and philosophy to which there is no good answer as long as God is conceived to intervene in the universe on behalf of specific people. I also learned that the biblical God needed to be put on trial at Auschwitz for crimes against humanity and called into account by conviction for those crimes(see Ellie Wiesel's *Trial of God*). In Heschelian terms, both God and humans are in partnership and have responsibilities toward each other. God, if not a verb, is an impossible concept to deal with. But since **there is no answer to theodicy,** I attempt to actualize the phrase *carpe diem* (seize the moment).

5. "And what difference does that make?"[93]

I learned from *Catch-22* the futility and *absurdity of war as a metaphor for the absurdity of life.* There is a secondary theme in this book. **Life is absurd, but one must carry on.** That, dear reader, is the sum of my entire life.

6. "I was a victim of a series of accidents, as are we all."[94]

I learned from *The Sirens of Titan* that **life is random**, but while life may be absurd, there is room for compassion ... even if it is to provide a soothing illusion. Sometimes life is so difficult that people need illusions just to get through it. Reality is very harsh. But if we can find ways to be compassionate to the sufferings of others, we may be able to bring some salve to our fellow travelers in life ... as well as to ourselves. **The truth will make you free, but first it will make you miserable. Yet, without hope, there is no life.**

7. "Which one is the patient?"[95]

I learned from the *Absurd Healer* that **systems make people well or ill** and that the community is the object of treatment to create conditions that can foster well-being or illness for individuals. I also learned that social justice is as much a part of health as is physical well-being. Who is the patient? The community is the patient. We separate ourselves from our families, friends, and communities at our own peril. Without my family, friends, and community, I would not have gotten as far as I did.

We cannot be alone in life.

8. "When you seek it, you can't find it."[96]

I learned from *Zen in the Martial Arts* that the arts are about life and not just about fighting. The martial arts are vehicles for understanding ourselves and the world. And I learned that one should not force things, and that going along with the course of things and remaining "consistent within one's own self" is the best way to *strive* to be in the world.

Zen combines Tao and Buddhism. As such, all of the themes of those two disciplines come into one melding of quietism and the acceptance of emptiness, the concern for suffering, compassion, and the idea of letting things take their course. Acceptance is a tough path. The Zen paradox is that when striving toward a goal, the goal may only be attainable by not striving. This is true for Tao as well.

When you seek it, you cannot find it.

9. "For then we would know the mind of god."[97]

I learned from *A Brief History of Time* that everything is not as it might seem to be (sounds like Alice in Wonderland) and that understanding the universe is not for the faint of heart. The universe is a complex, counterintuitive, and spooky (Einstein's word) place about which we can only best hope to make our models of understanding better and better, based on the data and evidence available. You just cannot answer questions like "Why is there something rather than nothing?" without considering physics, not just philosophy or theology. And you really need math to get it. I could get the concepts fairly well, but I always was abashed that I did not have enough math. And the more I learn about the universe, the less I really know.

We can strive to understand the universe but only with humility as to the boundaries of our understanding.

10. "I die in peace but not pacified, conquered and beaten but not enslaved, bitter but not disappointed, a believer but not a supplicant, a lover of God but not His blind Amen sayer."[98]

I learned from *Yosl Rakover Talks to God* the *power of faith still requires the necessity of calling the deity into account,* if there is indeed a deity that intervenes in the universe to change the laws of physics on behalf of people. Not even God can be allowed to disregard his own covenant with his own people or anyone else. One sees in *Yosl Rakover* the extreme struggle faith has with theodicy, the partnership between humans and God that Abraham Joshua Heschel has spoken so eloquently about. And if we and God are in partnership in the same universe, then we must hold ourselves to account for evil too. Blaming God might be a cop-out from blaming ourselves. Everyone is accountable … even God. The role of the Jewish people (and of humankind) is **to call out evil** and not just stand by in silence.

11. "Do not spread (false) rumors among your countrymen." "Whoever shames his neighbor in public, it is as if he has shed blood."[99]

I learned from *Words That Hurt, Words That Heal* the *power of the spoken word* and how careful we must be in order to increase well-being and decrease suffering, even through our speech. My father always used to tell me to "put the brain in gear before you put the mouth into action." That is a positive virtue to strive toward. Just like learning to let things take their course and other such lessons described above, controlling one's mouth is no easy process. Ultimately, we can only do the best we can. We can *strive* to be more aware and less hurtful. But forgiveness will always be a necessity and sincere apology a salve.
Watch your mouth!

12. "What are we to do with this knowledge?"[100]

I learned from *Who Wrote the Bible?* that even in religion, and even in literature, *facts outweigh myths and legends,* and the ability to recognize the differences between facts and myths takes courage and strength of mind.

Also, the idea that we cannot understand something by taking it out of context is a critical piece of understanding historical and rhetorical scholarship.

My studies of higher text criticism have had the effect of finding a deeper and richer sense of the text and our relationship to it.

But, in the end, ***"The truth will make you free, but first it will make you miserable."***

13. *"There can be no doubt that religious faith remains a perpetual source of human conflict."*[101]

An End of Faith teaches that we need to be realistic about the role of religion in our lives so as *not to spread myths and legends as if they were facts.* In fact, we need to be truthful with ourselves on all accounts. A dosage of healthy skepticism can be a helpful thing.

Doubt is not a bad thing when used in the service of logic and finding the truth. Cynicism, however, is not of any particular assistance.

I learned that ***It is a sin to lie to others, but it is a greater sin to lie to ourselves.***

14. "My mother always warned me not to think I could predict or control the future."[102]

I learned from *The Drunkard's Walk* that we need to be humble in the face of success or failure *because* the world operates through randomness and probabilities over which we have less power and control than we might wish to admit or want.

Randomness still does not remove from you the obligation to strive to be a better person.

15. I learned through this exercise that fourteen books are only invitations into much more in-depth study and that learning is indeed a lifelong enterprise. When I was a youth, a renowned Boston physician gave me a saying that has been with me my entire life: *"Learn as if you were to live forever, and live as if you are to die tomorrow."* I think I was always better at the first part than the second. But both are true and valuable to a good life.

16. Lastly, and consistent with the title of this work, "Striving is everything." As the angels sing at the end of Goethe's *Faust*, "Saved is the noble spirit from the bosom of the grave. Whoever strives to save himself, he can we save"[103] (my translation). A paradox exists in that striving itself may interfere with the outcome.

All we can do is our best to be kind and compassionate to all living things, to work toward the reduction of suffering and the increase of well-being ... and to forgive ourselves.

So, in sum, my journey to date has yielded these learnings which I try to carry with me:

1. An individual has the power to effect change.
2. Behavior rests on factors of which we are not always aware.
3. How does one strive while letting go of striving and outcomes?
4. There is no answer to theodicy (while God is conceptualized as a noun).
5. Life is absurd but we must carry on.
6. Without hope there is no life.
7. We cannot be alone in life.
8. When you seek it, you cannot find it.
9. We can strive to understand the universe but only with humility as to the boundaries of our understanding.
10. We must call out evil and not stand silently by.
11. Watch your mouth.

12. The truth will make you free but first it will make you miserable.

13. It is a sin to lie to others but it is a worse sin to lie to ourselves.

14. Randomness does not relieve you of the obligation to strive to be a better person.

15. "Learn as if you were to live forever. Live as if you were to die tomorrow."

16. All we can do is our best to be kind and compassionate to all living things, to work towards the reduction of suffering and the increase of well-being ... and to forgive ourselves.

AFTERTHOUGHT: WHAT IF THERE WAS ONLY ONE BOOK?

For some time, I have wondered about this question. What should I carry with me to refer to? I used to carry the Constitution of the United States. I used to carry the *Tao Te Ching*. I used to carry the *Kol Yaakov Siddur*. These are all wonderful and important texts. But surprisingly, I think that book might be *Words That Hurt, Words That Heal* by Rabbi Joseph Telushkin.

The reason I am tempted to select this book is because it really encompasses so much of what I strive for, value, and have such a hard time accomplishing. I was a victim of rough speech as a child, and it had a very negative effect on me into adult life. I have used bad talk and have been hurtful to people. I do not like suffering or diminishing well-being. Lashon harah (evil speech) can do that. We all do it. We all gossip. We all lie. We all diminish others. We are all talebearers. While it is just not right, it is a facet of human behavior. And it is a facet worthy of attention and striving toward correction.

Is it possible that the Holocaust might not have happened if Christians did not falsely accuse the Jews of such things as blood libels over centuries? Is it possible that courts of law might look like different institutions if people told the truth? Is it possible that some marriages might be saved if the parties did not malign each other? Is it possible that we might find more pleasure in life than existential despair if we spoke words of caring to one another? Is it possible that racism, sexism, and all the other isms that diminish people could be overcome if only we spoke well of one another?

I believe it is possible that the entire course of human history could have turned out differently if only humans did not bite one another with their words.

I am not suggesting that "love your fellow as yourself" is the prescription for well-being. Maybe I would feel differently if the statement said, "Respect your fellow as you would wish to be respected." Love is too hard. Respect is more important, in my opinion. And one way to show respect is not to say bad words to one another about one another.

I have a feeling that the Buddha missed this by placing such emphasis on nonattachment (although he certainly stressed "right speech"). I think that Lao Tzu may have overlooked basic human nature by placing such emphasis on noninterference.

The Torah commands the Israelite people not to tale-bear (Leviticus 19:16). It tells the story of how Aaron and Miriam were punished for their negative speech about Moses' "Cushite" (Ethiopian) wife (Numbers 12:1–15). The Jerusalem Talmud relates the statement that "The gossiper stands in Syria and kills in Rome" (Talmud Yerushalmi Peah 1:1). The Babylonian Talmud tells us that "Whoever shames his neighbor in public, it is as if he shed his blood" (BT Bava Metzia 58b). There is also the Rabbinic story (Midrash) that the reason for the destruction of Sodom and Gomorrah was not based on their sexual immorality but rather on their being fraudulent with each other in business.

For all of these reasons and more, I select *Words That Hurt, Words That Heal* as the one book of most importance to me of all of the books I have cited.

As a final comment, we must also be gentle with ourselves when we speak to ourselves in our own minds. This is the internalization of the bad words we may have heard that others have said to or about us. *To be a whole person, we must strive to treat ourselves just as well as we strive to treat others.*

TAKEAWAYS FOR MY PROGENY

I would take from all of this some words about striving for my children and grandchildren:

- There is no intrinsic meaning to life other than to live, be kind, and be compassionate.
- *Strive* to control what you say about people and not to cause suffering.
- *Strive* to reduce suffering and to increase well-being for all living things.
- *Strive* to be a rational and logical person.
- *Strive* toward excellence.
- *Strive* to be an intellectual. It really is okay to be an intellectual.
- *Be proud* of your heritage as a member of the Jewish people.
- Learn how to defend yourself both intellectually and physically.
- "Learn as if you are to live forever. Live as if you are to die tomorrow."
- "It is not for you to finish the work, but neither is it for you to desist from it."
- Try to be a good parent and grandparent. These are the most important jobs you will have in life.

Papa Stu

- Love the woods and the waters. Be close to nature.

Still hiking the Quabbin Reservoir at seventy (2017)!

- Make sure to have some fun.

At a Red Sox game

"Striving is everything," as the old German saying goes ("strebend ist alles"). You may not accomplish the goal, but the only ones who lose are those who never try. Rabbi Tarfon reminded us that "It is not for you to finish the work, but neither is it for you to desist from it."[104] No one has to have the expectation of being perfect.

I would also reflect on my theo-philosophy. I have found a rational resolution to my concern for the theodicy question. There is no answer as long as we conceive of God as a noun that intervenes in the laws of physics on behalf of certain people for his own reasons. Rather, God may be conceived of as a verb, the very process of the universe unfolding itself. God does not change the laws of physics because God is the laws of physics. "Everything happens as it must, not as it should."[105] I am comfortable with this answer to theodicy.

I believe in the God of Spinoza, of Einstein. I do not identify myself as an atheist because I am totally in awe of everything, and everything is my definition of God. "Ayn od milvado," says the Hebrew scripture,[106] "There is nothing besides God."[107]

Spinoza was called the "god-intoxicated man." I imagine myself in the same manner. There can be no spiritual self without *awe*. Following awe is a sense of *thankfulness* for being a self-conscious sentient being who can experience awe. I think that, for Jews, spirituality also entails *hope*. Without hope, there is no life. And finally, for Jewish spirituality, there must be both *action* and an *intention* toward holiness. Everything can be holy if attended to in a manner of awe and appreciation. Action elevates the mundane and ordinary to the position of holiness if we allow ourselves the intentionality of righteousness, of fairness, of justice, and of compassion for all things.

I guess that leaves the last expression of this self-reflection to be the same as Daniel Pearl at the end of his life … **"I am Jewish"** (and everything that implies about living life).

PS. Nothing lasts forever.

Take care of one another.

I love you.

Dad/Papa/Stu

EPILOGUE

The Revelation of Somni 451

To be is to be perceived, and to know thyself is only possible through the eyes of the other. The nature of our immortal lives is in the consequences of our words and deeds that go on and are pushing themselves throughout all time.

Our lives are not our own. From womb to tomb, we are bound to others past and present, and by each crime and every kindness, we birth our future. (Somni 451)

David Mitchell, *Cloud Atlas,* 2004, Sceptre, UK
Cloud Atlas, a film directed by Tom Tykwer, Lana Wachowski, and Lili Wachowski, 2012

APPENDIX A

Aphorisms

My mother was the queen of aphorisms. I myself am not bad at quotes. Many I have distilled from my books and literature. Some I have acquired from others. I thought it might be of value to identify some aphorisms and quotes of meaning to me, just as I did books. These are aphorisms and quotes I use often, and my friends know these as "Stuisms." I tried to keep them brief, but I do think that they give some additional flavor to understanding me and my journey. They are in no particular order:

1. "The masses are asses."(Al Forman. My father did not suffer fools lightly. My sons and I inherited that trait.)
2. "When you think it is not about money, it is about money." (Al Forman, paraphrasing H. L. Menckin; "When someone tells you it's not about money, it's about the money."[108])
3. "Justice, justice you will pursue."[109]
4. "Learn as if you are to live forever. Live as if you are to die tomorrow." (A renowned Boston physician and neighbor of a high school friend of mine.)
5. "The truth will make you free, but first it will make you miserable."(Charlie Barnes, PhD)[110]
6. "It is not for you to finish the work, but neither is it for you to desist from it." (Rabbi Tarfon[111])
7. "Pray for the welfare of the government, for without it men would eat each other alive."[112] (Pirke Avot)

8. "I hide myself in the thicket of the law, lest I fall in the winds that l blow outside."(I have not been able to attribute this quote to Sir Thomas More, but that is how I remember learning it.[113])

9. I would rather be kind than smart.[114]

10. I would rather be a reed that bends in the wind than a tree that breaks. (Zen saying)

11. "If I am not for myself, who will be for me? And if I am only for myself, what am I? And, if not now, when?" (Hillel[115])

12. "When you seek it, you cannot find it."[116](Zen saying)

13. "When the student is ready, the master will appear." (Zen saying)

14. "Speak up, judge righteously, champion the cause of the needy and the poor." (Proverbs 31:9[117])

15. "The world stands on three things, on truth, on judgment, and on peace." (Avot[118])

16. "Man is not a rational animal, he is a rationalizing animal."[119]

17. "I am a victim of a series of accidents, as are we all."[120]

18. "If I have seen farther, it is because I stood on the shoulders of giants." (Sir Isaac Newton[121])

19. "...chance favors only the prepared mind." (Louis Pasteur[122])

20. "Everything comes to those who wait." (Al Forman)

APPENDIX B

"The Righteous Man Stays the Course Despite the Difficulties"
by Ken Hartnett, *New Bedford Standard Times—*
Southcoast Today, January 6, 2008

(Ken Hartnett is the editor emeritus for the *New Bedford Standard Times*. When I retired from my position as president and CEO at the Greater New Bedford Community Health Center, Inc., he wrote this article about me. It was one of the greatest honors I have had in my life, to be thought of as Ken described. So, I include it herein.)

The righteous man stays the course despite the difficulties.

Here's a philosophically tinged question to begin the new year. Who in this faction-ridden city by the sea has been the most effective over the past 20 years in gaining the greatest good for the greatest number of people--- without great material benefit for themselves?

Now, I am talking New Bedford here, not the bosky suburbs. And I am not talking about people who built personal fortunes as part of their civic portfolio. Now, there's a purpose beyond personalities to this exercise. Maybe if the list can be narrowed down to a precious few we'll be able to figure out how they did it.

The more I thought about it, the more I thought about one low-profile chap who stepped down voluntarily just three months ago as head of the Greater New Bedford Community Health Center. I thought about Stuart I. Forman, age 60, now engrossed full-time in Jewish studies.

Stuart I. Forman used to drive me a little batty.

Probably few people in Massachusetts know more about the immense problems of health care delivery and how they are exacerbated by poverty than Dr. Forman does.

Yet, try to get the man to say something pithy that you can build a column around. Forget about controversy, contention or nasty cracks. Forget the unkind quote, on or off the record. What Dr. Forman would provide were servings of the ancient Hebrew sages, a heaping of quotations from the Talmud. As ancient Judaic sage Rabbi Tarfon reminded us: "It is not up to you to complete the work, yet you are not free to desist from it."

Now I have more than a little Thick Mick in me. But, suddenly, a light turned on the other day as I pondered Rabbi Tarfon's words.

Eureka!

That's how Dr. Forman does it. That's his secret. He is a righteous man who applies his beliefs to his work. He invokes words of the ancient sages for one reason: He lives by them. It is as simple as that.

In downtown New Bedford, under his direction, a comprehensive community based health complex has gradually evolved and is spreading substantially south from Elm Street, offering quality care to all comers, regardless of ability to pay. And, relatively few, outside of the thousands of New Bedford people who depend on the health center, seem to notice.

The amazing thing is that, as far as I know, in all the years of building, no one has even tried to stand in his way: not City Hall with all its potential roadblocks, not the business community, and certainly not the medical establishment, centered in Southcoast Hospitals and Hawthorn Medical Associates.

Not only did Dr. Forman get the bricks and mortar in place; he quietly helped get political victories, as well, including passage of the local referendum on fluoridated water.

But, not once, as far as I know, did Dr. Forman intrude, inflate, embarrass, bushwack, or ego trip, All he did was get things done, which is one reason he was awarded this newspaper's Man of the Year award in 2006.

Now cynics can say he succeeded because the medical establishment was eager to help and let someone else handle the care of poor people, the better-off patients who are more likely to live in suburbia than in the inner city.

It's hardly a coincidence that Stuart Forman is on the SouthCoast Hospitals community benefits committee. Who better?

I talked with him for two hours or more on the phone the other day. He talked about the great issues of American health care and how a society driven by money can meet the health needs of those without it; he talked about economically stratified health delivery systems and how they came into being, driven to a degree by necessity; he talked about the need for "black bottom lines" if American medicine is going to progress; he also talked about the importance of how those black bottom lines are directed: Does it go to institution aggrandizement or to serve the people? He talked about the need for preventive care and health education programs that reach the poor; he talked about the "architecture" of health care and its utter complexity. Only reluctantly did he talk about himself, and he was chagrined at the idea that I would write about him as opposed to his center and his board.

And again and again, the conversation swung back to ethics, to the duty he feels a Jewish man to reflect in his life and his work the values of his religious traditions.

"If we don't take care of each other, I don't know who else is going to take care of us," he says.

In the best possible world he believes, there would only be one level of care for everyone regardless of income.

But, we live in the real world, not the ideal one, and New Bedford is no different from many other places in America, where almost 46 million people are without health care, despite the existence of a nationwide network of community health centers like the one downtown.

To move closer to a more ideal system will require getting the various parts of the health system, the profits, the non-profits, the community based groups, the doctors, the administrators, the private and public sectors, with all the varying agendas, to work more in tandem to "bring into being one super architecture" offering quality care to those who need it.

That won't happen anytime soon; it might not happen at all. But, that's where the Rabbi Tarfon's words come in: The righteous man is not free to desist from the job at hand.

Dr. Forman is pursuing Jewish studies through the Spertus Institute of Chicago as a way to help him get better at his secular mission as a health professional. He plans to return to his field as a consultant or manager when he completes his studies.

Those studies had been on the shelf for 40 years. He was eager to pursue rabbinical studies as a young man but took a different direction because of family considerations.

"This is not a leaving (of my field) but an enhancement," he says. "If I didn't take that opportunity now, I would regret it. It is something I wanted as a kid. I didn't do it, and if you have an opportunity to do what you didn't do and don't take it when you can, then shame on you. So, I decided to take this leap of faith.

Dr. Forman says he is free to focus on Jewish studies because he had completed his own personal mission: helping create a one-stop, multifaceted health center to serve all who need it.

He left me with a quotation, this one from another sage, Rabbi Hillel: "If I am nothing to myself who will be for me. And if I am for myself only, what am I? And if not now, when?"

Maybe the whole city should take Jewish studies. Maybe we'd work together for a change.

Ken Hartnett's 2008 article's text above is printed herein with the written permission of the Local Media Group, Inc. d/b/a the *Standard Times*.

GLOSSARY OF TERMS

Akhenaton: Pharaoh of the eighteenth dynasty in Egypt who introduced monotheistic worship of the sun.

Aggadah: These are the stories, parables, and legends within the Talmudic text.

Amidah: The prayer known as the Eighteen Benedictions. When Jews refer to "prayer" within the prayer service, they mean the Amidah.

andragogy: Pedagogy is teaching of children, and andragogy is teaching of adults.

apikoros: A Greek word found in the Talmud for "heretic."

Aron Kodesh: The holy ark or cabinet found in the synagogue, which contains copies of the Torah.

Ashkenazim: Jews of Eastern European origin.

Aveyrah: a sin, a bad deed.

Azazel: The scapegoat upon which the high priest would ritually confess the sins of the Israelite people once a year on Yom Kippur. The goat was then removed from the community and sent off into the wilderness.

Baruchu: The Jewish Call to Prayer. ("Praised is G-d, the Exalted One. Praised is G-d, the Exalted One, in the World forever.")

Baruch Hashem: Thank G-d!

bimah: This is a Greek word meaning "platform." Today it refers to the elevated lectern and stage from which the Jewish worship service is conducted, including the reading of the Torah.

blood libel: The false accusation that Jews kidnapped Christian babies to drain their blood to bake matzot at Passover.

BPHC: Bureau of Primary Health Care, US Public Health Service.

bracha: Hebrew for "blessing." The formula of most brachot begins "Blessed art Thou our Lord our G-d, King of the Universe, who ..."

Bubbe: "Grandmother" in Yiddish.

Bowenian: Murray Bowen, PhD, was the father of family systems theory at Georgetown University. Bowenian refers to his theories, which include the process of multigenerational differentiation as a process of maturation of self. This includes setting boundaries between where the child begins and ends and where the parent begins and ends. In Bowenian theory, differentiational boundaries reduce anxiety. Everything I learned about Murray Bowen came from his student Charles Barnes, PhD (and of course Bowen's books).

chavurah: a gathering of friends for study or spiritual activities.

chaver/chaverim/chaverei: are Hebrew terms for friend, male friends, and friends without sexual reference, respectively. The term is also applied to study partners.

CHC: Community health center.

Chevrutah: A dyad of students. A style of Talmud study.

chutzpah: Unmitigated assertiveness. Chutzpah has been described as when you kill your mother and father and throw yourself on the mercy of the court as an orphan!

daven: Yiddish for "praying."

differentiation of self: This is a Bowenian family system theory construct that means figuring out where you begin and end and where everyone else (especially those in the family or origin) begin and end. It is the process of self-definition. The higher the level of definition of self, the less anxiety, and the lower the level of definition of self, the higher the anxiety.

Ehbester: A Yiddish name for God.

Einsatzgruppen: These were (volunteer) "police" who followed the Nazi troops in their invasion of Eastern European countries and were tasked with murdering the Jews of the invaded communities. Generally, this was done by shooting men, women, and children at close range and burial of their naked bodies in mass graves. Later, shooting was determined to be too expensive, and the Nazis began gassing masses of people at concentration camps.

El Moley Rachamim: "God full of compassion," a Jewish prayer of remembrance of the dead.

endocarditis: An infection of the heart.

excommunication (Jewish): Jewish excommunication was a decree by a rabbinic court that prohibited people from doing business with a particular heretic or allowing that person to worship together with other Jews. Baruch Spinoza was excommunicated in the seventeenth Century in Amsterdam for challenging the Mosaic authority of the Torah. In the eighteenth century, a rabbinic court in Vilna, Lithuania, excommunicated the entire Hasidic Movement.

FQHC: Federally qualified health center. This is a specific designation under federal law that acts as a form of accreditation. FQHCs are designated under Section 330 of the Community Health Act of 1968. The act mandates local control over healthcare delivery by CHCs.

frum: A Yiddish word for observant.

Gilgamesh: Ancient Sumerian myth that includes a flood story predating Noah and the Hebrew flood legend.

Gödel's incompleteness theorem: The1935 theory of Kurt Gödel that proposed that one cannot prove all truths and that no system can prove itself.

Halakah: This word refers to the corpus of Jewish law and jurisprudence as expressed in the Babylonian Talmud and in the *Code of Jewish Law* by Joseph Caro and emended by Moses Isserlis to include Ashkenazi traditions.

Haskalah: The Jewish Enlightenment of the eighteenth to twentieth centuries, reflecting the European Enlightenment of the eighteenth and nineteenth centuries CE.

Heisenberg uncertainty principle: The 1927 theory of Werner Heisenberg that showed that one cannot tell the exact position and momentum of a subatomic particle at the same time.

Holocaust: The term for the systematic killing of six million Jews and another five million Russians, Poles, homosexuals, Freemasons, and many others by the German Nazis and their associates in WWII.

hootnanny: A gathering of folk musicians to play music impromptu together.

Hyksos: Canaanite tribes who went to Egypt and became rulers there for two centuries until a civil war expelled them. They lived in Goshen in Egypt and returned to Canaan. Josephus, the Jewish Roman historian, felt that the Israelite tribes were the Hyksos in Egypt, as the Joseph story in the Torah and the Hyksos stories appear so compatible.

JCAHO: The Joint Commission on Accreditation of Healthcare Organizations is a critically important accreditation requiring a very serious level of organizational management and integrity.

jeet kune do: This is Chinese for "way of the intercepting fist" and the title of the book on martial arts by Bruce Lee.

Judaism: the religion of the Jewish people, generally considered being monotheistic.

> **Conservative Judaism**: That denomination of Judaism that tries to conserve the Halakah while accommodating itself to modernity.
>
> **Hasidism**: Various sects of Orthodox Judaism that depend on the Kabbalah and on Rebbiism. Some scholars feel that Hasidism tends toward pantheism. The sect was originally established in 1760 by the Baal Shem Tov (Master of the good name). Other sects of Hasidism grew over time to include the Breslev, the Chabad (Lubavitch), the Satmar, and others. The sects also formed scandalous heretical messianic sects, such as the Jacob Frankists and the followers of Shabbati Zvi.
>
> **Hubus**: Humanistic Judaism is secular atheism for Jews.

JuBus: Jewish Buddhists. I have no idea what this means other than an expression of New Age something.

Orthodox Judaism: The form of Judaism thatis dependent of Jewish law of the Halakah of the Talmud.

Reconstruction Judaism: A form of Judaism that believes that the Jewish people are a civilization and that the Halakah are actually customs and folkways of the Jewish people.

Reform Judaism: That denomination of Judaism that rejects the ritual Halakah in favor of moral law in accommodation to modernity. It is very concerned with social justice. It believes that Judaism is a religion rather than a nation.

Renewal Judaism: Judaism based on tradition/Halakah and spirituality expressed in music. It also is concerned with social justice.

Workman's Circle Judaism: Socialist/Communist unionist internationalism thatuses Yiddish as its lingua franca and is attached to the Jewish people but is secular and atheist.

Judenrein: This German word literally means "Jew pure" and refers to a community in
which the Nazis had exterminated all of the Jews who had lived there.

Jujitsu: A form of martial arts that's tresses throws, joint locks, and chokeholds.

Kabbalah: A form of mystical Judaism that traces its origins to the *Zohar* (Book of Splendor) which is a mystical text upon which Kabbalism is based. One of the best studies of the Kabbalah is found in the book by Gershom Scholem, *Major Trends in Jewish Mysticism.*

Kaddish: The Jewish prayer in praise of G-d said during mourning, after completing a section of the worship service and after formal textual study.

Kedushah: This prayer is a section within the Amidah that is in praise of Hashem. Christians know the part of the Kedushah within their liturgy as "Holy, holy, holy ..."

Kenpo: A form of martial arts that combines elements of both Chinese and Japanese martial arts, created by Professor Chou in Hawaii.

Kiddish: Jewish blessing on wine.

Kotel: The holiest shrine in Judaism located in Jerusalem. It is the remnant of the Western Retaining Wall for the Temple Mount that was built by King Herod.

lehn: This is a Yiddish word that literally means "study" or to "learn." It is applied to chanting the Torah text as a part of the Jewish worship service.

Litvak: A Jew who comes from either Lithuania or one of the Baltic states.

Masada: This was Herod's desert palace that Zealots escaped Jerusalem to during the first Roman War in 68–72 CE. They withstood Roman attacks and siege for four years, at the end of which the thousand-person community committed suicide rather than be taken captive by the Roman legion.

me'ah: This word means "one hundred" in Hebrew. The Me'ah program at Hebrew College in Newton, Massachusetts, is an adult learning program of one hundred hours of Jewish study over a two-year period.

Mechitzah: This is a physical separation between men and women used during the worship service in the Orthodox and Hasidic traditions. It is never used in egalitarian Judaisms.

Meshebeyrach: The Jewish prayer for wellness and healing.

mezuzah: The biblical text commands the Israelite people to write the divine laws on their doorsposts of their houses. The mezuzah is a box or cylinder that contains a scroll with those divine commands on it. It is not a talisman. It is a memory device.

minyan: A quorum of ten necessary for Jews to pray the "Holy words" (The *Barachu* or the Call to Prayer, *Kedushah* prayer within the Amidah or Eighteen Blessings, and *Kaddish*). Only the Orthodox and Hasidim only count men for the minyan. All other denominations of Judaism are egalitarian. Some of the Reform will say Kaddish without a minyan.

Mitnagdim: Those Jews opposed to the Hasidic Movement.

Mitzvah: a good deed, fulfilling a biblical commandment.

monotheism: The theology that there is only one god.

Nostra aetate: The statement on the relationships of the Catholic Church with other religions.

Pantheism: The theology that everything is god.

Panentheism: The theology that god is in everything.

Pater familius: Latin for the "paternal head of the family."

Pesach (Hebrew)/Passover (English): The eight-day Torah-prescribed holiday commemorating the legendary Exodus of the Israelite people from slavery in Egypt. The first two and last two days of the holiday are work-prohibited holy days.

Pogrom: Violent attack on a Jewish community in Eastern Europe by local townspeople. These were common events in pre-WWII Eastern Europe. The Chmielnicki Massacres in 1648 in Poland killed one hundred thousand Jews.

Pyrrho: The first Greek philosopher to propose skepticism as a discipline of philosophical thought.

Rebbiism: Attachment to a Rabbinic master in an almost cultish attachment. A central factor to the Hasidic Movement.

Rosh Hashanah: The Jewish New Year in the fall season for people. The Talmud established three other new years for animals, for trees, and for the anointing of kings.

Rushashuk: A Jew who comes from the Russian Pale of Settlement of the Jewish people.

sacrificial cult: The religion of biblical Israel, which included animal sacrifice.

Schrodinger's cat: A thought experiment proposed by Erwin Schrodinger that showed that one could not know anything with certainty but only with probabilities until a phenomenon is observed directly. A foundation of quantum physics.

secularism: Secularism is the indifference to religion and the dependence on logic, math, and science in the search for truth. The path to Western secularism, in my humble opinion, leads from Pyrrho to Socrates, to Aristotle, through Copernicus, Spinoza, Darwin, Marx, Freud, Wellhausen, Heisenberg, Schrodinger, and Gödel. I suppose that one could throw in the existentialists for good measure.

Sephardim: Jews of Spanish origin and, by extension, Jews of the Mediterranean rim.

Shabbat: The Jewish Sabbath, which begins at sundown of Friday night and goes until sundown of Saturday evening.

Shabbat lichts: Sabbath lights in Yiddish. Jews ceremonially enter the Shabbat by lighting two candles and saying a bracha.

Shavuoth: The spring Torah-prescribed holiday symbolic of the receiving of the Ten Commandments at Mt. Sinai by Moses.

Shimini Atzeret: The last holy day of the eight-day period of Sukkoth.

Shoah: Hebrew for "Holocaust."

shtetl: A Jewish village.

shul: In Yiddish, "shul" means school. It is used to denote a synagogue.

Simchat Torah: The celebration at the end of Sukkoth of ending and beginning of the reading of the Torah for its annual cycle.

Socialism: My own definition of socialism does include the concept of class warfare and oppression of the working class by the bourgeoisie, equalization of a society's income through the redistribution of wealth through an aggressive graduate income tax, the provision of free public education, a program of social welfare to care for all members of society at a basic level of well-being, and the regulation of the marketplace. In my definition, I do not agree with the total control of the means of production by the state. I do not approve of the communist concept of violent revolution to obtain the destruction of the economic class system, because I do agree with anthropologist Clyde Kluckhon that violent revolution only changes faces and does not change processes.

Sukkoth: The fall harvest festival prescribed in the Torah. It is also the holiday that commemorates the legendary wandering in the desert for forty years after the Exodus from slavery in Egypt. The holiday is eight days long, with the first two and last two days being work-prohibited holy days.

Ta'aseh and Lo'ta'aseh: These are biblical Hebrew terms for to-do and not-to-do commandments in the Torah. A to-do commandment begins "You shall," and a Lo'ta'aseh commandment begins "You shall not ..."

tallit: Prayer shawl used by men in the Orthodox tradition and by both men and women in other denominations of Judaism.

tallit gadol: This is a large form of tallit.

Talmud: The Talmud consists of the Mishnah (c. 100 BCE–200 CE), which has statements of Jewish law and the Gemara (c. 200 CE–500CE), which elaborates on the Mishnah. There are two Talmuds, the Jerusalem Talmud and the Babylonian Talmud. The Babylonian Talmud has authority in determining Jewish law.

Tanak (TANAK): This is an acronym for the twenty-fourbooks of the Jewish canon known as Torah (the fivebooks of Moses), Neviim (Prophets), and Ketuvim (Writings). These comprise the Old Testament, or the more politically correct term, the "Hebrew Scriptures." It does not include the Book of the Maccabees or any of the pseudepigrapha.

Tao: Pronounced "Dao," this Chinese word means "way" or "path."

tayku: Aramaic term for "there is no answer."

tephillin: Phylacteries. These are unique to Judaism and Jewish worship. They are leather boxes ritually bound to the forehead and left arm (if you are right handed) and that contain scribed sections of the Torah laws.

theodicy: Theodicy is the question of how a compassionate and merciful god can allow evil and suffering to exist in the world.

Tisha B'Av: The ninth day of the Hebrew month of Av is when the Second Temple in Jerusalem fell to the Romans in 70 CE. Other great tragedies of the Jewish people have been lumped into this "holiday" to make it the worst day of the Jewish year. The Book of Lamentations is read on that day while people sit on the floor or hard benches in signs of mourning.

Torah: This term is generally used for the five books of Moses. It also is used for the Tanak or the twenty-four books of the Jewish canon. More contemporarily, the term may be used euphemistically to refer to the entire corpus of Jewish literature, jurisprudence, and theology.

Transubstantiation: The Eucharist. This is a Christian ritual during a service when people eat a wafer and drink wine that is understood to respectively become the actual body and blood of Jesus and allows the communicant to both remember and commune with Jesus.

Trinitarianism: The Christian theology that God has three Godheads (Father, Son, and Holy Spirit) comprising a single deity.

tzedakah: Charity.

Yom Kippur: The Jewish Day of Atonement, a communal day of fasting and repentance.

Zen: A form of Buddhism that combined Taoist and Buddhist principles brought to Japan in the fourteenth century.

Zionism: The belief and political philosophy that the Jewish people require a homeland in the land of Israel with Jerusalem as its capital.

z"l: Zachar l'brachah; "of blessed memory."

BIBLIOGRAPHY/ REFERENCES

Alport, Gordon. *The Nature of Prejudice*. New York: Doubleday Anchor Books, 1958.

Alynski, Saul. *Rules for Radicals*. New York: Random House, 1972.

Ayer, Alfred Jules. *Language, Truth and Logic*. New York: Dover Publications, Inc.

Ayer, Alfred Jules. *Probability and Evidence*. New York: Columbia University Press, 1972.

Armstrong, Karen. *Fields of Blood, Religion, and the History of Violence*. New York: Alfred A. Knopf, 2015.

Aurelius, Marcus. *Meditations*. London, England: Penguin Classics, 2006.

Bartlett, John, Kaplan, Justin general editor. *Familiar Quotations*. Boston/NY/London: Little Brown and Company, Sixteenth Edition, 1992.

Brenner, Charles, MD. *An Elementary Textbook of Psychoanalysis*. Garden City, NY: Doubleday Anchor Books, 1957.

Berlin, Adele, and Marc Zvi Brettler, ed. *The Jewish Study Bible*. Oxford, NY: Oxford University Press, 2004.

Bowen, Murray. *Family Therapy in Clinical Practice*. New York: Jason Aronson, Inc., 1985.

Bronfman, Edgar. *Why Be Jewish, A Testament*. New York: Twelve, Hachette Book Group, 2016.

Campbell, James. *The Power of Myth*. New York: Anchor Books, 1991.

Camus, Albert. *The Myth of Sisyphus.* New York: Vintage International, 1991.

Caplan, Gerald. *Principles of Preventive Psychiatry*. New York: Basic Books, 1964.

Carroll, James. *Constantine's Sword*. New York: Mariner Books, 2001.

Carroll, James. *Practicing Catholic*. HoughtonMifflin, NY, 2009.

Churchland, Patricia. *Braintrust*. New Jersey: Princeton University Press, 2011.

Cooper, David, Rabbi. *God is a Verb*. New York: Penguin Books, 1998.

Constitution of the United States, New York: Fall River Press, 2012.

Darwin, Charles. *The Origin of Species*. (First published edition 1859). New York: Bantam Classics, 2008.

Dasgupta, Partha. *Economics, A Very Short Introduction*. Oxford, United Kingdom: Oxford University Press, 2007.

Dawkins, Richard. *The Blind Watchmaker*. New York: Norton and Company, 1986.

Deming, Edward; *Out of the Crisis*. Cambridge, Massachusetts: MIT Press, 1982.

Dumont, Matthew, P. MD. *The Absurd Healer*. New York: The Viking Press, 1968.

Fab, Joe et al. *Paper Clips*, 2004.

Fisher, Roger and William Ury, with Bruce Patton, ed. *Getting to Yes*. Boston/New York/London: Houghton Mifflin Company, 1991.

Forman, Stuart I. and Stephen Havas. "Massachusetts Post-traumatic Stress Disorders Program; A Public Health Model for Vietnam Veterans". *Public Health Reports*. March/April 1990.

Frank, Otto. *The Diary of Anne Frank*. New York: Modern Library 1952.

Freud, Sigmund. *Moses and Monotheism* (First edition 1937) New York: Vintage Books, 1967.

Friedman, Richard Elliot. *Who Wrote the Bible*. New York: Harper & Row Publishers, 1979.

Fromm, Eric. *The Art of Loving*. New York: Bantam Books, 1956.

Fulcher, James. *Capitalism, A Very Short Introduction*. Oxford, United Kingdom: Oxford University Press, 2004.

Goldstein, Baruch, Rabbi. *For Decades I Kept Silent*. Tuscaloosa: University of Alabama Press, 2008.

Goldhagen, Daniel Jonah. *Hitler's Willing Executioners*. New York: Vintage Books, 1997.

Grandon, Temple. *Animals Make Us Human*. Boston/New York: Mariner Books, 2009.

Hyams, Joe. *Zen in the Martial Arts*. New York: Toucher/Putnam Books, 1979.

Harris, Sam. *An End of Faith, Religion, Terror and the Future of Reason*. New York: W.W. Norton &Co., Inc., 2004.

Harris, Sam. *Letter to a Christian Nation*. New York: Vintage Books, 2006.

Harris, Sam. *Free Will*. New York: Free Press, 2002.

Hawking, Stephen, *A Brief History of Time: From the Big Bang to Black Holes*, NY, Bantam Books, 1988.

Hawking, Stephen and Leonard Mlodinow. *The Grand Design,* Bantam Books, NY, 2010.

Hawking, Stephen with Leonard Mlodinow. *A Briefer History of Time*. New York: Bantam Books, 2008.

Heinlein, Robert. *Stranger in a Strange Land*. New York: G.F. Putnam's and Sons, 1961.

Heinlein, Robert. *Assignment in Eternity*. New York: Baen Publishing Enterprises, 2012.

Heller, Joseph. *Catch 22*. New York, New York: Dell Publishing Co., 1961.

Herman, Arthur. *The Cave and the Light*. New York: Random House, 2014.

Heschel, Joshua Abraham. *Man is Not Alone.*, New York: The Noonday Press, 1951.

Heschel, Joshua Abraham, Susannah Heschel, ed. *Moral Grandeur and Spiritual Audacity*. New York: Farrer, Strauss and Giroux, 1996.

Hoffer, Eric. *The True Believer*. New York: Harper Perennial Modern Classics, 1951.

Hoffer, Eric. *The Ordeal of Change*. New York: Harper and Row, 1963.

Hyams, Joe. *Zen in the Martial Arts*. New York: Penguin Putnam/ Random House, Inc., 1979.

Jung, Carl. *Man and His Symbols*. Garden City, New York: Doubleday & Company, 1964.

Kamenetz, Rodger. *The Jew in the Lotus*. New York: HarperCollins, 1995.

Kehati, Pinchas. *Mishnah Avot*. Jerusalem,Israel: Eilner Library, Department for Torah Education and Culture in the Diaspora.

Kennedy, Caroline. *A Patriot's Handbook*. New York: Hyperion, 2003.

Kolitz,Zvi. *Yosl Rakover Talks to God*. New York: Vintage Books, 1999.

Kopp, Sheldon. *If You Meet the Buddha on the Road, Kill Him*. New York: Bantam Books, 1976.

Kopp, Sheldon. *An End to Innocence*. New York: Bantam Books, 1978.

Lathem, Edward Connery ed. *The Poetry of Robert Frost*. New York: Henry Holt Company, 1969.

Lao Tzu. *Tao Te Ching*. New York: Barnes and Noble Classics, 1997.

Lazare, Aaron. *On Apology*. New York: Oxford Press, 2004.

Lee, Bruce. *The Tao of Jeet Kune Do*. Santa Clara, California: Ohara Publications, 1975.

Lifton, Robert Jay. *The Nazi Doctors*. New York: Basic Books, Inc., 1986.

MacLeish, Archibald. *JB*. Boston, Massachusetts: Houghton Mifflin Co., 1958.

McKeon, Richard, ed. *The Basic Works of Aristotle*. New York: The Modern Library/Random House, 2001.

Melville, Herman. *Moby Dick*. New York, New York: Signet Classics, New American Library.1961.

Michaelson, Jay. *Everything is God, The Radical Path of Non-dual Judaism*. New York: Schocken Publishers, 2009.

Millard, Nellie D., Barry G. King, and Mary Jane Showers. *Anatomy and Physiology*. Philadelphia and London: W. B. Saunders Co., 1956.

Mlodinow, Leonard. *The Drunkard's Walk, How Randomness Rules Our Lives*. New York: Vintage Books, 2009.

Mlodinow, Leonard and Deepak Chopra. *War of World Views*. New York: Harmony Books, 2011.

Nagel, Thomas. *What does It All Mean? A Very Short Introduction to Philosophy*. Oxford, United Kingdom: Oxford University Press, 1987.

Newman, Michael. *Socialism, A Very Short Introduction*. Oxford, United Kingdom: Oxford University Press, 2005.

Nichols, Mike. Screenplay by Buck Henry. *Catch 22*, 1970.

Okakura, Kakuzo. *The Book of Tea*. Boston, Massachusetts: Shambala Publications, 1993.

Pew Research Center. *A Portrait of American Jews*. www.Pewforum, October 1, 2013.

Plato. *The Republic*. New York: Barnes and Noble Classics, 2004.

Plato. *Essential Dialogues of Plato*. New York: Barnes and Noble Classics, 2005.

Pearl, Judah and Ruth eds. *I Am Jewish*. Woodstock, Vermont: Jewish Lights Publishing, 2004.

Prothero, Steven. *Religious Literacy. New York:* HarperOne, 2007.

Prothero, Stephen. *God is Not One*. New York: HarperOne, 2010.

Rand, Ayn. *Atlas Shrugged*. New York: Signet Books, 1957.

Rawls, John. *A Theory of Justice*; Revised Edition. The President and Fellows of Harvard College, Cambridge, Massachusetts: The Belknap Press of Harvard University, 1999.

Rovelli, Carlo. *Seven Brief Lessons on Physics*. New York: Riverhead Books, 2014.

Rovelli, Carlo. *The Order of Time*. New York; Riverhead Books, 2018.

Russell, Eric Frank. *Wasp*. United Kingdom: Dobson Books Ltd., 1957.

Sartre, Jean Paul. *Anti-Semite and Jew*. New York: Schocken Books, 1948.

Sartre, Jean Paul. *No Exit*. New York: Vintage Books, 1946.

Scherman, Noson Rabbi and Rabbi Meir Zlotowitz, co. eds., *The Complete Artscroll Siddur, Siddur Kol Yaakov, Nusach Ashkenaz*. Brooklyn, New York: Mesorah Publications, Ltd., 1988,

Sheleg, Yair. "A Living Talmud Encyclopedia", *Ha'aretz* (Israel), Feburary 2, 2008.

Simek-Downing, Lynne and Stuart I. Forman. "The Teaching of Substance Abuse; A National Survey and Residency Curriculum", *Substance Abuse*. Association for Medical Education and Research in Substance Abuse, Winter 1987.

Spielberg, Steven. *Saving Private Ryan*. 1998.

Telushkin, Joseph, Rabbi. *Words That Hurt. Words that Heal*. New York: Quill/ William Morrow; 1996.

Thompson Clara, MD, Milton Mazer, MD and Earl Wittenberg, MD, eds. *An Outline of Psychoanalysis.* New York:The Modern Library, 1955.

Tolkien, J. R. *The Hobbit.* United Kingdom: George Allen and Unwin, 1937.

Tolkien, J.R. *The Lord of the Rings.* United Kingdom: Allen and Unwin, 1954.

Terkel, Studs. *Working.* New York: Avon Books, 1974.

Vonnegut, Kurt. *Slaughter House Five.* New York: Dell Publishing Co., 1969.

Vonnegut, Kurt. *The Sirens of Titan.* New York: Dell Publishing, 1959.

Wade, Nicholas. *The Faith Instinct.* New York: The Penguin Press, 2009.

Walton, Mary. *The Deming Management Method,* New York: Perigee Books, 1986.

Watts, Allen and Mark Watts, ed. *The Way of Zen.* Novato, California: New World Library, 2000.

Watts, Allen. *What is Tao?.* New York: Vintage Books, First Vintage Spiritual Classics Edition, 1999.

Wiesel, Eli. *The Trial of God.* New York: Schocken Books, 1979.

Wells, H. G. *History of the World, Vol. 1 and 2.* Garden City, NY: Doubleday and Co., 1961.

Wine, Sherwin T. Rabbi. *Judaism Beyond God.* KTAV Publishing House, Inc., Society for Humanistic Judaism, Milan Press, 1995.

Wittgenstein, Ludwig. *Tractatus Logic-Philosophicus.* Barnes and Noble, 2003. Originally published 1922.

Yankelovitch, Peter and William Barrett. *Ego and Instinct.* New York: Vintage Books, 1971.

Yutang, Liu. *The Wisdom of Laotse.* New York: The Modern Library, 1948.

Zinn, Howard. *A People's History of the United States 1492-Present,* Revised and Updated Edition. New York: HarperPerennial, 1995.

Note: Not every book referenced herein in this bibliography has been specifically mentioned within the text itself. However, all books in this bibliography have informed the preparation of this manuscript.

ENDNOTES

1   Referred to hereafter as *A Brief History of Time*.

2   Referred to hereafter as *An End of Faith*.

3   Referred to hereafter as *The Drunkard's Walk*.

4   Archibald MacLeish, *JB* (Boston, MA: Houghton Mifflin Co., 1958), 11.

5   Kurt Vonnegut, *The Sirens of Titan* (NY: Dell Publishing Co., 1959), 233.

6   Ibid, 233.

7   Carlo Rovelli, *The Order of Time* (NY: Riverhead Books, 2018), 178.

8   Ibid.

9   Anne Frank, *The Diary of a Young Girl* (NY: Modern Library, 1952), 278-279.

10 Eric Frank Russell, *Wasp* (UK: Dobson Books Ltd., 1957), 9

11 John Bartlett, Justin Kaplan, general editor. *Familiar Quotations* (Boston/NY/London: Little, Brown and Company, Sixteenth Edition, 1992), 281. A quote by Sir Isaac Newton in a letter to Robert Hooke, February 5, 1676.

12 Charles Brenner, *An Elementary Textbook of Psychoanalysis,* (Garden City, NY: Doubleday Anchor Books, 1957), 4.

13 Bowenian systems theory recommends understanding one's parents as individuals if one is to differentiate oneself from the parents. Differentiation of self is a family systems goal construct.

14 John Bartlett, Justin Kaplan general editor. *Familiar Quotations* (Boston/NY/London: Little, Brown and Company, Sixteenth Edition, 1992), 301. "The proper study of mankind is man.", Alexander Pope, An Essay on Man: Epistle II.

15 Liu Yutang, *The Wisdom of Laotse* (NY: The Modern Library, 1948), 305.

16 Archibald MacLeish, *JB* (Boston, MA: Houghton Mifflin Co., 1958), 4.

17 Ibid, 11.

18 John Bartlett, Justin Kaplan, general editor. *Familiar Quotations* (Boston/NY/London: Little, Brown and Company, Sixteenth Edition, 1992) 457. "In Memory of Arthur Henry Hallum." Alfred Lord Tennyson, 1850: "Nature, red in tooth and claw."

19 My grandfather was a traveling salesman. Originally, I called him Pop. When he would come home from his long road trips, I would say, "Hi, Pop!" The name became one word and stuck forever as "Hipop."

20 Joseph Heller *Catch 22* (NY,NY: Dell Publishing Co.,1961), 17.

21 John Bartlett, Justin Kaplan, general editor. *Familiar Quotations* (Boston/NY/London: Little, Brown and Company, Sixteenth Edition, 1992), 492. "War is hell." General William Tecumseh Sherman

22 Kurt Vonnegut, *Sirens of Titan* (NY: Dell Publishing Co., 1959), 233.

23 My uncles, Hyman and Morris Forman, were in the Battle of the Bulge. They actually met in combat. Morry was in the infantry pinned down by the Germans. Hy was in Patton's Third Army, which relieved the infantry. Hy's tank hit a land mine. He was severely wounded, and his war was over. Morry's unit broke out of the bulge and proceeded on to win the war in Germany. Neither ever talked about their experiences. My cousin complied Uncle Hy's letters home, which illuminate some of that action.

24 Kurt Vonnegut, Sirens of Titan (NY, NY: Dell Publishing Co,1959), 233.

25 I heard this quote from my good friend Dr. Charles Barnes.

26 Dumont, Matthew P., *The Absurd Healer,* The Viking Press, NY, 1968, pg.10.

27 Ibid, 39.

28 Ibid, 10.

29 Matthew P. Dumont, *The Absurd Healer* (NY: The Viking Press, 1968), 39.

30 Ibid, pg. 81.

31 This was President Bill Clinton's campaign mantra.

32 Joe Hyams, *Zen in the Martial Arts (NY:* Penguin Putnam /Random House Inc., 1979) 21.

33 The infamous boxer Joe Lewis is reported to have said this phrase to his opponent in a title fight.

34 Stephen Hawking, *A Brief History of Time from the Big Bang to Black Holes* (NY: Bantam Books, 1988), 175.

35 Schlicht was killed by a Nazi student and Carnap escaped the Nazis to teach in the USA, thus ending the Vienna Circle and its work, c. 1933.

36 Zvi Kolitz, Carol Brown Janeway, translator, *Yosl Rakover Talks to God* (NY: Vintage Books, 1999), 23.

37 Pew Research Cente*r, A Portrait of American Jews,* www.pewforum.org, October 1, 2013.

38 Daniel Pearl was a secular Jewish journalist covering the war in Afghanistan. He was captured by the Taliban. Before they decapitated him with a knife, his last words were "I am Jewish." His family wrote the book *I Am Jewish* in commemoration of Daniel Pearl. They interviewed many Jewish people, old and young, rich and poor, scholarly and not, and complied their answers to

what his statement means to them into this book. It is a serious book and worth reflecting upon.

39 Eva Fleischer ed., *Auschwitz: Beginning of a new Era?* Participation by Emil Fachenheim, held at the Cathedral of St. John the Divine, NYC, June 1974, (NY: KTAV Publishing Co., 1977).

40 Zvi Kolitz, Carol Brown Janeway, translator, *Yosl Rakover Talks to God,* (NY: Vintage Books, 1999), 23.

41 Ibid.

42 Rabbi Baruch Goldstein, *For Decades I kept Silent* (Tuscaloosa, AL: University of Alabama Press, 2008).

43 Archibald, MacLeish, *JB* (Boston, MA: Houghton Mifflin Co., 1958), 11.

44 Depending on the source, it has been reported that Mohammud may have killed those who fought against him including some 700 Jewish men who fought against him in Medina.

45 Pew Research Center Religion and Public Life, www.pewforum.org. 2015.

46 Joe Fab et al, *Paper Clips*, 2004.

47 Rise of anti-Semitic incidents in the USA and around the world is well documented in the current public media worldwide.

48 Jay Michaelson, *Everything is God; The Radical Path of Nondual Judaism,* (Boston & London: Trumpeter Books, 2009), 95

49 Adele Berlin, and Marc Zvi Brettler, eds., *The Jewish Study Bible* (Oxford/NY: Oxford University Press, 2004), Lev 19:16, 254.

50 ibid, Prov 31:9, 1486.

51 Nosson, Scherman and Meir Zlotowitz, eds., *The Complete Artscroll Machzor for Yom Kippur* (Brooklyn, NY: The Artscroll Mesorah Series, 1986), 134. Vidui Confessional. Note: Jews tend to speak in the plural, having a national god rather than a personal god.

52 Rabbi Joseph Telushkin, *Words That Hurt. Words That Heal,* (NY: Quill/ William Morrow, 1997), 14.

53 Ludwig Wittgenstein was one of the greatest philosophers of the twentieth century. His book *Tractatus Logico Philosophicus* (NY: Barnes and Noble Co., 2003) examines our use of language.

54 Pinhas Kehati, *Mishnah Avot,* (Jerusalem, Israel: Eilner Library) 69. Pirke Avot, Chapter 3, Mishnah 2.

55 Richard Elliot Friedman, *Who Wrote the Bible?,* (NY: Harper and Row Publishers, 1979), 243.

56 Yair Sheleg, "A living Talmud encyclopedia" (Israel: Haaretz.com, February 14, 2008). David Weiss Halivni quote in his resignation letter to the Jewish Theological Seminary, 1983.

57 Benei Mitzvah is a term that is used for both males and females who are going through the rite of passage at thirteen years old of reading from the Torah.

58 Stuart I. Forman, and Stephen Havas, "Massachusetts Post-traumatic Stress Program: A Public Health Model for Vietnam Veterans": *Public Health Reports*, March/April 1990.

59 Lynne Simek-Downing and Stuart I. Forman, "The Teaching of Substance Abuse: a National Survey and a Residency Curriculum", *Substance Abuse*: Association for Medical Education and Research in Substance Abuse, Winter 1987.

60 Kurt Vonnegut, *The Sirens of Titan* (NY: Dell Publishers,1959), 233.

61 Sam Harris, *An End of Faith, Religion, Terror and the Future of Reason* (NY: W.W. Norton And Co., 2001), 236.

62 Ontological proof: the existence of the universe implies the existence of a creator god.

63 Cosmological proof: since everything is contingent on everything else in terms of cause and effect, the universe must be contingent of a creator god.

64 Marx, Karl, *A Contribution to the Critique of Hegel's Philosophy of Right*, Deutsch-Franzosische Jahrbucher, 1844.

65 An adage that I think I learned from Charles Barnes, PhD.

66 This derives both from the work of Jay Michaelson and David Cooper. If God is everything and God is a verb (the process of the universe), then God is the laws of physics.

67 Jay Michaelson, *Everything is God, The Radical Path of Nondual Judaism* (Boston & London: Trumpeter Books, 2009), 95, 99.

68 Leonard Mlodinow, The Drunkard's Walk, How Randomness Rules Our Lives (NY:Vintage Books, 2009), 218.

69 Pinhas Kehati, *Mishnah Avot* (Jerusalem, Israel, Eilner Library. *Pirke Avot Chapter 4 Mishnah 15)* 129, "It is not within our hands(to explain) either the serenity of the wicked or the sufferings of the righteous."

70 Stephen Hawking and Leonard Mladinow, *A Briefer History of Time* (NY: Bantam Books, 2008), 93.
Stephen Hawking, *A Brief History of Time from the Big Bang to Black Holes* (NY: Bantam Books, 1988), 56.

71 Stephen Hawking had been commonly known to often quip that God not only did not play dice, he threw the dice under the table where you could not see them.

72 Fyodor Dostoevsky, Richard Pevear and Larissa Volokhonsky translators, *The Idiot* (NY: Vintage Classics, 2003), 382.

73 Ibid

74 John Bartlett, Justin Kaplan, general editor. Familiar Quotations (Boston/NY/London: Little, Brown and Company, Sixteenth Edition, 1992), 502. Louis Pasteur, Inaugural Lecture at the University of Lille, Dec.7,1854

75 Sheldon Kopp outlines these concerns throughout his books *If You Meet the Buddha on the Road, Kill Him* and *An End to Innocence.*

76 Matthew P. Dumont, *The Absurd Healer* (NY: Viking Press, 1968), 79.

77 Jay Michaelson, *Everything is God*, The Radical Path of Nondual Judaism (NY: Schochken Publishers, 2009), 95.

78 Pinhas Kehati, *Mishnah Avot* (Jerusalem, Israel: Eilner Library), Pirke Avot Chapter 4 Mishnah 15 tells us that "It is not within our hands(to explain) either the serenity of the wicked or the sufferings of the righteous.", 129.

79 Jay Michaelson, *Everything is God, The Radical* Path *of Nondual Judaism* (NY: Schocken Publishers, 2009), 99.

80 Matthew P. Dumont, *The Absurd Healer* (NY: Viking Press, 1968), 79.

81 Brooke Atkinson, ed. *Walden and Other Writings of Henry David Thoreau* (NY: Modern Library, 1931), 7.

82 Albert Camus, *The Myth of Sisyphus* (NY: Vintage International, 1991), 3.

83 Ibid

84 Archibald MacLeish, *JB,* (Boston, MA: Houghton Mifflin Co., 1958), 11.

85 Adele Berlin and Marc Zvi Brettler, *The Jewish Study Bible* (Oxford/NY: Oxford University Press, 2004, 2014), Deuteronomy 30:19, 415.

86 Albert Camus, *The Myth of Sisyphus,* (NY: Vintage International, 1991) 65.

87 Abraham Joshua Heschel, Joshua *Man is Not Alone,* (NY: Farrer, Straus and Giroux, 1951), 11.

88 Eric Frank Russell, *Wasp* (UK: Dobson Books, Ltd., 1957), 9.

89 Pinhas Kehati, *Mishnah Avot* (Jerusalem, Israel, Eilner Library), Mishnah 2 Chapter 16, 65.

90 Charles Brenner, *An Elementary Textbook of Psychoanalysis* (Garden City, NY: Doubleday Anchor Books, 1957), 4.

91 Liu Yutang, Liu, *The Wisdom of Laotse* (NY: Modern Library,1948), 305.

92 Archibald MacLeish, *JB,* (Boston,MA: Houghton Mifflin Co., 1959), 11.

93 Joseph Heller, *Catch-22,* (NY,NY: Dell Publishing Co., 1969), 17.

94 Kurt Vonnegut, Kurt, *The Sirens of Titan* (NY: Dell Publishing Co., 1959), 233.

95 Matthew P. Dumont, *The Absurd Healer* (NY: Viking Press, 1965), 16.

96 Joe Hyams, *Zen in the Martial Arts* (NY: Penguin/Putnam Random House, Inc., 1979), 21.

97 Stephen Hawking, *A Brief History of Time, From the Big Bang to Black Holes* (NY: Bantam Books, 1988), 175.

98 Zvi Kolitz, *Yosl Rakover Talks to God* (NY: Vintage books, 1999), 23.

99 Joseph Telushkin, *Words that Hurt. Words That Heal* (NY: Quill/ William Morrow, 1996), 16.

100 Richard Elliot Friedman, Richard Elliot, *Who Wrote the Bible?*, (NY: Harper and Row Publishers,1979), 243.

101 Sam Harris, *An End of Faith, Religion, Terror and the Future of Reason*, (NY: W.W. Norton & Co. Inc., 2004) 236.

102 Leonard Mladinow, *The Drunkard's Walk* (NY: Vintage books, 2009), 218.

103 Johann Wolfgang von Goethe, Walter Kaufman, translator, *Faust*, (Garden City, NY: Doubleday Anchor Books, 1963)

104 Pinhas Kehati, *Mishnah Avot* (Jerusalem, Israel: Eilner Library), Chapter 2 Mishnah 16, 65.

105 Jay Michaelson, Jay, *Everything is God, The Radical Path of Non-Dual Judaism* (Boston & London: Turmpter, 2009), 94.

106 Ibid, 50.

107 Ibid, 53.

108 www.goodreads.com

109 Adele Berlin, Adel and Marc Zvi Brettler, *The Jewish Study Bible*, (Oxford/ NY: Oxford University Press, Oxford, 2004), Deuteronomy 16:18, 383.

110 Charlie Barnes was my mentor as a psychotherapist, fishing buddy, and close friend. He was one of the most educated people I have known, having attended Harvard, Yale, and Georgetown Universities. He was a disciple of Murray Bowen and taught me virtually everything I know about family systems theory. Charlie was an ordained Methodist minister, having attended Yale Divinity School. I miss his advice, spirituality, and comradeship deeply.

111 Pinhas Kehati, *Mishnah Avot*, (Jerusalem, Israel: Eilner Library), Pirke Avot Chapter 2 Mishnah 16, 65.

112 Ibid, 67.

113 Undocumented attribution to Sir Thomas More.

114 Joseph Telushkin, *Words That Hurt. Words that Heal*; (NY: Quill/Willim Morrow, 1996) 126. "The great Jewish writer Milton Silverstein once said, "When I was young, I admired clever people. Now that I am older, I admire kind people."

115 Pinhas Kehati, *Mishnah Avot* (Jerusalem, Israel: Eilner Library), Pirke Avot Chapter 1 Mishnah 14, 27.

116 Joe Hyams, *Zen in the Martial Arts*, (NY: Penguin/Putnam/ Random House, 1979), 21.

117 Adele Berlin and Marc Zvi Brettler, *The Jewish Study Bible* (Oxford/NY: Oxford University Press, 2004),Proverbs 31:9, 1486.

118 Pinhas Kehati,Pinhas, *Mishnah Avot* (Jerusalem, Israel, Eilner Library), Pirke Avot Chapter 1Mishnah 18, 34.

119 Robert Heinlein,(*Assignment in Eternity* (NY: Baen Publishing Enterprises, 1949), 54.

120 Kurt Vonnegut, *The Sirens of Titan* (NY: Dell Publishing Co., 1959), 233.

121 Sir Isaac Newton

122 John Bartlett, Justin Kaplan, general editor. *Familiar Quotations* (Boston/NY/London: Little, Brown and company, Sixteenth Edition, 1992) 502. Louis Pasteur, Inaugural lecture at the University of Lille, December 7, 1854.

Printed in the United States
By Bookmasters